BEHIND THE CURTAIN

A Journey to Sobriety

Jean

 www.trafford.com

North America & international
toll-free: 1 888 232 4444 (USA & Canada)
fax: 812 355 4082

In memory of my cousin Pat Kern,
who was there for me all my life

And I would like to thank:

Anne Schuster, whose workshops started it all and without whom nothing would have been written at all. Maire Fisher, who encouraged and helped me all along the way. Ria Barnard, without whom I doubt the book would have seen the light of day. Alida Potgieter, for her understanding and encouragement.

And Mary Monaghan, Cheryl Leslie and Nicole Chidrawi. They know why!

And, of course my husband for his patience and my children and grandchildren for their interest and encouragement.

It is well I drew the curtain, thought I; and I wished that he might not discover my hiding place.
Jane Eyre by Charlotte Brontë.

Who has not sat, afraid, before his own heart's curtain?
Rainer Maria Rilke, *Duino Elegies*, "The Fourth Elegy", translated from German by Albert Ernest Flemming

PROLOGUE

I stand in the bay window behind the curtains. I shiver as I stand here. It is two o'clock in the morning. I can feel the cold tiles underneath my bare feet. My pyjamas are thin, but it is fear that makes me shiver. Joe has been beating my mother for at least the past hour.

His shouting and terrible swearing brought me from my bed to slip onto the stoep and to climb through the sitting room window where I can stand in the bay window, hidden by the curtains. I can't see, but I can hear what is happening to my mother. The darkness around me is cold, and I can smell Joe's sweat. The curtains smell of lavender and I wonder why. They are thick and lined so that the main light comes from the street lights outside.

I wonder if Joe can see my shadow, and my heart beats a little faster. If he sees me, he will lunge at the curtains and start to beat me too. When this happens, my mother always intervenes and tries to pull him away, desperately defending me. She tells me just to stay in my bed and feign sleep, so that Joe will leave me alone. But, surely, if she defends me, I should be allowed to defend her too?

The dreadful swearwords come out of Joe's mouth so loudly that I know the neighbours must be hearing them too. I wish that they would call the police. But none of them ever do.

"Bitch! You think I won't use this?"

I can't see, but I know he's got the axe again. The axe lies to one side of the fireplace and his threats are real. I am terrified, but I have to look. I have to find the courage to take a peek, to make sure of what is happening beyond the curtain. My mouth is dry and my limbs rigid from fear, so rigid that I cannot even tremble. I know that this could be the last night of my life. I am very cold. I understand the saying "frozen to the spot".

I peep. The axe is in his hand. He lifts it above his head. My mother stands on the other side of the table, head held high, looking him in the eye, daring him to do it.

I would like to be able to say that I caused some diversion to save my mother's life. My fear, my guilt, my very youth, kept me transfixed behind that lavender-scented curtain, unable to scream or move or even to think.

I was fifteen years old, and this had been happening to us since I was ten. Night after night I would lie in my bed, every muscle in my body tense. I could taste the blood in my cheeks as I bit them and held them between my aching jaws. I can't remember that it was painful, but I can still taste the blood. Night after night I would wait for the screaming to begin. And there weren't many nights that passed quietly, without a noisy, terrifying outbreak of violence and abuse. I really don't know what it was that I said or did, or how I said or did it, that was so wrong that it "set Joe off", as my mother used to say. I would lie there, struggling to understand what it was that I needed to do differently so that Joe would be pacified and stop his foul-mouthed physical abuse.

Joe didn't bring the axe down on my mother's head, but he did bring it down with a thunderous noise right onto the centre of the table. It hit with such force that it cleft the table in two.

CHAPTER ONE

THE BEGINNING

My very first memory embarrasses me. I am sticking pins into my uncle Frank's leg. He even gives me the pins to do it. I giggle, and so does he as I thrust the pins into his leg. He doesn't squeal with pain or even pull a face. Suddenly I feel a slap on the side of my head. It seems I have stuck a pin in the wrong leg. I burst into tears and run away, clutching my buzzing ear.

Uncle Frank had a wooden leg—and in those days artificial legs really were wooden and you could stick pins into them. I thought that both his legs were like that. What did I know about wooden legs? I was not quite three years old. The slap he gave me was very painful. My head swam and my eyes watered. I felt very much to blame—and that I deserved that slap.

I am not sure whether it was this incident that triggered my removal from the care of Uncle Frank to the care of the local crèche, but I suspect that it might have been. We lived in Pretoria, and so it was somewhere in the suburbs of that city that I attended the crèche.

One very cold Sunday morning during the time that I was at the crèche, my parents had a fire going in the living room. My father had just put the poker in the fire to freshen it up a bit. The phone rang, and he left the poker in the fire while he went to answer it. When he came back, he removed it and hung it on a hook next to the fireplace. It was red-hot, and I grabbed it with my right hand, saying, "What a pretty thing."

I was rushed to hospital, where my burns were treated. As young as I was, I wondered why we didn't go straight home afterwards. Instead, we went to the Railway Club in Pretoria, where my parents sat drinking while my hand throbbed terribly and I wanted nothing more than to be cuddled and nursed, or to lie down on my own bed.

I remember little about the crèche, except my very last day there. My mother came straight from the school where she was teaching at the time to fetch me. She found me cleaning up my own sick—undigested green beans that I had deposited on the floor of the reception area, as I had been unable to reach the lavatory in time. I remember my mother shouting at the staff and being very angry with them. She scooped me up in her arms, gathered my things and took me away. I never saw that crèche again. It was such a comfort to have my mother hold me close, not blaming me for what had happened, but rather demonstrating clearly that she didn't believe that it had been my fault. I nuzzled into her neck and felt loved and protected. My mother started a search for somewhere she could leave me and know that I was safe and properly cared for while she was at work.

When I was three years and nine months old, I started my school career at an Anglican convent in Pretoria, where the sisters were reluctant to take me in, perhaps because I was so young. I remember having my photograph taken because I was the smallest and youngest child they had ever had at the school. The photograph of me with the head girl of the day was to be the frontispiece of the school magazine, with the caption "Our top and tail".

The photograph was taken in front of the imposing school building—designed by Sir Herbert Baker. I found the school friendly, and the gardens were beautiful. My favourite place was a sunken garden, called "Sleepers" because the benches were old railway sleepers. The little girls had a hedgehog there that they kept as a pet. It was a good place to keep it because it couldn't get out, yet had a large area in which to roam and feed.

There was no preschool facility, and so I just sat in the classroom with the grade ones. At the end of the year I found myself in grade two. I loved being there. I enjoyed the schoolwork, and the older girls treated me like a little mascot.

When I was five, my father joined the army and lived in barracks, preparing to be posted to the war zone. I can remember visiting him on Sundays, taking picnic lunches of bacon and egg, or cheese and onion pies. Dad would sit in the car, reading the newspaper. Mom would snooze on the rug spread out under a tree. I used to read the paper over my father's shoulder and surprised him one day by reading out loud: "The Russians say that this is due to technical difficulties." My father was astounded and remarked to Mom that it must be a jolly good school they had found for me!

Everything seemed peaceful, and I was happy with my parents.

Eventually my father was sent "up North" to join the troops in Egypt. I can remember a period when we stayed alone, my mother and I, in a little house situated in a panhandle, tucked away behind someone else's house. My mother was gentle and kind and played Peggoty and Hangman and did puzzles with me.

I am not quite sure exactly when Dad left to fight in Egypt, but I do know that he kept in touch with me by means of letters and postcards. I remember how once, before he left, he rushed to my bedside when I was very ill, with a dangerously high temperature.

My father was a kind and intelligent man, who had left school early in order to take a job to help pay for his younger brother and sister to go to university. He returned to school when he was much older than the usual age for matriculants. He survived the unkindness of his fellow pupils and obtained his matric with flying colours. It was strange for me to hear his better-educated siblings speak of him in a superior fashion, denigrating him for not being as educated as they were.

Those lonely times couldn't have been easy for my mother. I think that she began to rely quite heavily on her "sundowner" each evening and, although I didn't realise it then, it was probably during this time that she gradually began drinking more. I suppose those "sundowners" gave her some of the warmth and comfort she must have been missing.

In those days married women were only able to get temporary teaching appointments, so my mother asked the school to take me in as a boarder because she was often away teaching in rural areas. Before I turned six I was in boarding school.

4

I struggle to knot my tie. I wish Sister Constancy would come and help me. I don't know why she hasn't come today. I'm going to have to tie my shoelaces next, but I am afraid to try. Where is Sister Constancy this morning? She comes into the dormitory every morning to help me get dressed.

The dormitory is big, and I am alone in my little cubicle. I leave the tie and the shoelaces. Maybe Sister Constancy will still come to help me.

It is a struggle to make the bed. I can't reach behind it to tuck in the blankets, so I just leave them as they are. As long as the bits of the bed that can be seen look tidy, I won't get into trouble with Matron. I wonder if Matron tidies my bed for me sometimes. I think it looks better in the afternoons than it does in the mornings.

I miss my mother terribly.

CHAPTER TWO

IT IS HARD FOR EVERYONE

The thread of my years at boarding school runs through my life as a saving grace. School was a place of safety and routine, a place where things were always the same and where I knew that I was loved and nurtured. Some of the best memories that I have are of my time at school. Memories of time spent there—it was home to me for a long time—are still important to me, and things that happened there often gave me a sense that there was a place where I belonged and where people cared about me.

Temporary teachers didn't get paid in the school holidays and had to take other temporary jobs if they wanted a regular income. I remember one holiday job that my mother took in 1938, just before I went to boarding school.

The foundation stone of the Voortrekker Monument in Pretoria was being laid. Afrikaners came from far and wide to attend the celebrations. What Mom and I had to do was to be photographed with these people in front of the foundation stone. I'm not sure whether I was part of the original deal or whether Mom persuaded the photographer to let me be there so that she didn't have to leave me with a baby-sitter.

The exciting thing was that we were dressed in Voortrekker costume: long dresses and kappies. My outfit was yellow, I think, and my mother's a pale green—not that the colours mattered, because in those days there was no colour photography anyway.

I occasionally wonder whether any of these photos still exist and whether there are folk that look at them and ask their granny who those people are.

Mom was sent to teach in farm and country schools in places that didn't offer her companionship, and there was seldom a library or a reading population around at all. Her dreams must have been shattered. I do believe that these circumstances fed her need to drink more and more, to dull the loneliness and the feeling that perhaps there wasn't going to be much more for her in life. There wasn't much available to keep her busy and fulfilled—certainly no theatres, although I do remember that there was sometimes a local "bioscope", as the cinemas were called, and occasionally the circus came to town.

I recall one occasion when the circus came by. I was on holiday from school and I stayed with her in a godforsaken dorpie, Pienaarsrivier, in the Northern Transvaal. She was excited about being able to go to the circus that night and she told me about the clowns and the trapeze artists. We set off expectantly—just across the road from the hotel, in fact, and found our seats in the big top.

I recall the blare of the brass band assailing my ears and inducing the first fearful beats of my heart. Then followed the entrance of the clowns, one enormously tall and one small and round. They had big white eyes and round red noses, with feet that were obscenely large, over which they stumbled and threatened to fall.

I let out a shrill, terrified scream and started to bawl, causing everyone to turn and look at me. My mother grabbed my hand and literally dragged me out of the opening in the tent and across the road to the veranda of the hotel. There she flopped down on a bench, firmly pulling me down to sit beside her. Her anger and disappointment were palpable. It was my fault that she would miss the circus. I lay down and put my head in her lap. She touched my hair and while I buried my face in her lap, crying, she watched the performers as they came out at the back of the tent after each act. To this day I feel guilty about what happened that night.

She once had to teach in a rural village for two terms. The village was Roedtan in the Northern Transvaal. It was a real backwater dorpie. She told me how the train had stopped miles from the village at eleven o'clock at night. The guard had walked with her in the dark, carrying her suitcase to the house where she was to board with the headmaster. The train waited patiently at the siding for the guard to return.

How frightening it must have been to undertake that walk in the dark through a strange landscape, guided by a stranger. What an inauspicious start to her new job. Yet Mom was never one to be intimidated. My memories of her are all with head held high.

When my mother knocked, the meester's wife opened the door, took one look at her and shouted, "No more juffrouens are going to stay here, thank you! Go and find another place. You are all Jezebels, out to steal my husband." And with that she slammed the door.

Luckily the guard had relatives in the village, a Mr and Mrs Young, and he took my mother there. The Youngs willingly took her in—in return for a fair sum for board and lodging.

The place was comfortable, but the food was terrible. At her first meal, my mother was offered a tempting plate of soup. As she put the first spoonful to her lips, her landlady warned her: "Be careful of the bones, Juffrou, the doves were very young when I took them out of the nest." No more soup.

What was really good to eat was the bread that Mrs Young baked, so Mom existed on that, buying herself tomatoes and cheese, cold meats and tinned fish to go with it.

Early one morning the man of the house was stamping around, muttering to himself. Mrs Young called out, "What are you looking for, Dolf?"

"A handkerchief. I'm going out shooting," he replied. Upon which his wife called to the maid in the kitchen, "Lenie, bring the bread cloth!" She handed her husband the cloth she used to cover the rising bread dough. That night it was back in place, spotted with blood. No more bread for poor Mom! She bought her own from then on.

"Please, Mommy let me come. Please, Mommy!"

I was terrified, crying and clinging to my mother. She was very angry with me and pushed me back into my bed. Mrs Young was shouting at her to come quickly.

"Just leave her, Elizabeth!" she yelled to my mother. "She's just naughty."

I was choking with fear. I was afraid that my mother would leave and I would never see her again. I was not naughty; I was just afraid that Mommy wouldn't come back again. I was always afraid that I would be left alone, with no one to care for me.

I don't think at the time I was really conscious of the fact that my mother was drinking heavily, although she often smelled of something with which I was not familiar. This made me feel very insecure, and I developed a terrible fear of being left alone. If possible, I would follow my mother from room to room, making sure that I always knew where she was. On the night of the fire I recognised that smell and I could smell it on Mr and Mrs Young as well. I know today that the three of them must have been drinking. I was terrified that she would leave with them and not come back again. A scared child was probably the last thing she wanted clinging to her. I don't think she had ever had much freedom to do what she wanted to do or be who she wanted to be.

The flames from the big fires light up the sky. The peanut crops on the farm have caught alight and the sparks are jumping from one pile of harvested peanuts to the next. It looks like a fireworks display. I am afraid of fireworks too. I know this because Mommy's birthday is on Guy Fawkes Day and she always has fireworks for her birthday. I crawl under the bed when this happens, and she laughs at me.

The Youngs and my mother want to go out in their car to look at the flames and to see how far the fire has gone.

I want to go too. Being left alone in this house, where snakes have been found under the window seat, terrifies me. I am sure that going out where all those fires are is dangerous too. But I would rather be in danger from fire and have my mother with me than stay alone where the snakes are. It is my first holiday after being sent to boarding school and I want to be with my mother all the time.

Mommy grabs me and drags me by the hand to the car waiting outside. She bundles me roughly into the back seat and climbs in after me. Mr Young drives off while I sit sobbing. I am told that I am naughty and selfish and a big baby. I didn't think so before, but I am beginning to believe it now.

My school had three terms a year and the state schools where my mother taught had four. I spent the school term being nurtured and cared for in a gentle and genteel environment and joined my mother for my holidays, where I usually spent the days at the school where she was teaching, in the classroom of the grade that I happened to be in at the time.

The schools in which she taught were mostly Afrikaans medium, and I was soon fluent in the language. These were not bad days. I made many friends, even though these friendships lasted only for short periods. However, the difference in background and age set me apart from those children, as well as the fact that my mother was a teacher. I remained a lonely child who kept to herself.

CHAPTER THREE

LIFE BECOMES FRIGHTENING

I am eight years old. It's a Saturday morning during the school holidays, and Mom has an appointment at the hairdresser's. She sits in front of the mirror in the hairdressing salon. The hairstylist is twisting Mom's hair up in little bits of paper and then dousing it with lotion. The smell fills my nostrils, and I hate it. It stinks. I can't understand how my mother can bring herself to sit through this smelly ordeal. Is curly hair really worth it? My own hair is very straight, thin and floppy and, as much as I would like curls, I know I will never have it permed if this is the way it has to be done.

My mother whispers to the hairstylist, and immediately I prick up my ears to tune in to the conversation. She thinks that because she has lowered her voice I won't be able to hear what she is saying.

"My sister Maddie is getting divorced," she says.

My heart pounds in my chest. My poor cousin Pat. She's an only child, like me. What will happen to her? Where will she live?

My head is full of questions and I am afraid.

Perhaps they will just leave her at her boarding school? I imagine her all alone in the holidays, eating a lonely dinner at the long refectory table and sleeping all by herself without any other girls in the dormitory.

I remember that as a truly frightening moment. Adults tend to forget that children hear and understand more than they think. As an only—and lonely—child, I was well practised in "listening in", eavesdropping, picking up the news that grown-ups shared with each other but never with a child.

It was on another of those warm and sunny Saturday mornings a few months later that I heard my mother's voice, in conversational mode, saying, "Do you remember what I told you a few months ago? About my sister Maddie? Well, the same thing is happening to me." This time my heart seemed to stop altogether.

Whenever I visit a hairdresser and sit in a chair and look at myself in the mirror, I remember how I heard the news that my parents were to be divorced. I felt insecure and vulnerable—feelings that were to stay with me for a very long time.

When she eventually broke the news to me, my mother told me that my father didn't want us any more. My father told me that he wanted me to live with him, but he felt that it was better for a girl to be with her mother. I was utterly confused and didn't know whom to believe.

In the back of my mind was the knowledge that, since he returned from Egypt, I had several times heard my father angrily accusing my mother of drinking too much. I remember hearing an argument between my parents. My father said, "I believe you are an alcoholic, Elizabeth. We can't carry on like this." She didn't reply. She just kept on crying. I had never heard the word "alcoholic" before and although I wasn't quite sure what it meant, I knew enough to think that this might be why my father had asked for a divorce.

I had remained in boarding school after my father's return, and I realise now that it was probably because of my mother's drinking that it was thought best that I stay there.

I believe that it was at this time that things started to get financially difficult for both my parents. I don't know what a divorce cost in those days, but they weren't well-off to begin with, so the additional costs of moving into two different dwellings and dealing with the attendant problems must have been difficult.

When my father told me that he wanted me to live with him but that a girl needed her mother, I felt that he was suggesting that my mother didn't want me either, though he never said it in so many words. He kept in touch with me and told me that as soon as he was settled, I would be coming to spend holidays and weekends with him.

Self-confidence and a sense of self-worth don't grow out of circumstances like these, and I became a secretive, unhappy child. Although I experienced times of serenity and love at school with the sisters and also with my mother's extended family, I came to believe that I could rely only on myself. Apart from school, there didn't seem to be anything in my life that was solid and dependable. I lived in a cocoon, never sharing my fears and concerns with those around me. I lived in fear of being abandoned. I was afraid that the vision I had had in that hairdressing salon of my cousin—alone, abandoned and unloved—would become my reality.

School came to be a place where I always felt safe. There was no doubt in my mind that I was "wanted" there. The gentle nuns truly cared for us, and I still wonder how they managed to do as well as they did despite the fact that none of them had ever had children of their own!

It was an Anglican convent—very "High Church". Incense was used during the celebration of the Eucharist, there was wonderful Gregorian chanting in the chapel, and the Angelus bell rang every day at noon. There was a lightness and a joyfulness about what we were taught, and this extended to the way in which the girls were handled. There was no teaching of death and damnation, nor were we ever given the idea that we were unworthy. The school motto was "Daughters of the King"—which other schools regarded as being somewhat "weird"—but we had no doubt that it referred to our being loved and accepted by "God the Father". This was important to me and made me feel that I was a member of a family and was cared for and appreciated.

CHAPTER FOUR

A HAPPY TIME
AT HOME

When I was nine, my mother got a teaching post at Kilnerton Institution near Silverton, just outside Pretoria. It was a Methodist mission school. My mother and her younger sister taught there. The school was known as "The Black Eton" because many well-known and successful black people, such as Nthato Motlana, were educated there during the 1940s and 1950s.

Kilnerton was on the outskirts of Pretoria at the time. Today the city has grown beyond where the school used to be and, if it still existed, it would be right in the middle of the suburb that I think is now known as Kilnerton.

The days at the mission school were happy. There were many grown-up parties and the school choir would sing for the guests. It was there that I was introduced to "Nkosi Sikelel' iAfrika", sung a capella in three or four parts, usually in the outdoors under the stars.

I had a spell of not being a boarder. We lived in a big, high-ceilinged house with a huge kitchen and a walk-in pantry. I believed that it also had a ghost, and my mother was convinced of it too. One evening, as we sat in the sitting room, she shivered and said that she had seen an old man with a dog walk past the door and down the passage.

The house was large and had a big, tree-filled garden with a wide drive that wound around a circle of lawn in the front. I learned to ride my bicycle there, round and round the driveway. I can remember the sense of freedom I had as I spun around that circle. I loved the green space provided by the big trees around the house. The mission was situated on several acres of land and I could ride my bicycle wherever I liked. It was surrounded by farmland and just across the railway line from our house was Smith's Farm, where the children from the mission were allowed to play on the huge haystacks. We climbed them with difficulty, sliding down and climbing up again until we reached the top. From there we could see all around us: the mission, the houses, the railway station.

Smith's Farm offered not only haystacks, but also cows, chickens, pigs and horses. I can still feel the warm satisfaction it gave me to stroke the horses' necks and feel them wetly nuzzle a piece of apple from the palm of my hand; and the warm satisfaction of lying snugly in a haystack with a book that often fell into my lap while I watched the birds in the trees and in the sky above me.

My cousins and I crouch on the steps below the veranda. It is dark there and no one is aware of us. We take in the fine clothes of the guests and strain our ears to hear what they are talking about. Every time a waiter goes past, we grab something to eat off his tray. I like the bacon-stuffed prunes best, and a little heap of the toothpicks that spear them together is lying beside me. My uncle is home from the war on leave. He has been in the thick of things "up North". Tomorrow he is to go back, and this party is to say goodbye to him and to wish him a safe return.

The weather is perfect and I can see the stars. My cousins are giggling beside me. We are all a little fearful of being discovered. There is a warm buzz of conversation, and I hear the words "Tobruk" and "Montgomery". It is 1944.

The college choir arrives and takes its place. The voices soar into the dark sky, seeming to reach the stars. I feel peaceful and calm. Is there really a war somewhere? The stars are sending out a message of peace and hope.

People are raising their glasses and calling out, "Here's to a safe homecoming, Eddie," and "Let's drink to when we all meet again." I see my uncle's white teeth as he grins in the moonlight. He is happy with his family tonight and he must surely be thinking of when he will be back with us all.

He was killed in Italy a few months later. We never saw him again.

On the Kilnerton property there was a high school, a Teachers' Training College, as well as hostels and staff houses. Despite the ghosts, I believed that it was the safest place in the world. The only time we ever felt threatened was during the school holidays when the students were away.

I am trembling—cold and terrified in the early hours of the morning. My mother and I are alone in our house. The students are on holiday and my aunt and cousins are also away. We hear someone walking in the flower beds outside our bedroom window. My mother calls out a challenge—"Who's there?" Of course there is no reply, but we can hear someone there. I screw up my courage and peep through the curtains and see the shadow of a person just across the path that runs alongside the house.

Mom fetches the shotgun from behind the wardrobe. I am shocked and wonder if Mom even knows how to use it. "Where are the bullets?" Mom asks breathlessly. My heart is beating wildly. I tear the drawers out of the bedside table and scratch through them frantically. I see one bullet and grab it. I watch as my mother loads it into the shotgun and fires the gun through the window.

We phone the police, Mom dialling with trembling fingers, and we sit waiting. Everything is completely silent.

The police didn't come until after daybreak the next morning. We had been too afraid to leave the house, for fear of finding the intruder—either dead or alive. We never did find anything, although the policeman told us that there were footprints under the bedroom window.

In the light of the paranoia that gripped the country many years later, it may seem strange that we felt so safe while we were living at Kilnerton. Perhaps it was in those days that I began to understand that cooperation and respect among all the races in this country were essential for its success and well-being.

I was taught to respect all the people at that school. I always addressed the other teachers as Mr, Miss or Mrs. This was quite contrary to the way in which most whites spoke to black people, using only their first names.

I fondly remember Mr Serekoane, a teacher who lived next door to us. He gave my mother lessons in Sepedi and he would arrive humbly, hat in hand, at our back door when it was time for the lesson. It took us a long time to persuade him to come to the front door, as befitted a man of his status.

When the students were in residence, we didn't fear anything. A good example was one day when there was a raging highveld thunderstorm. The lightning was very close and struck a tree on the koppie behind us. The thunder crashed loudly, ominously and threateningly. Minutes later our back door burst open and in rushed four students, wet to the bone, exclaiming, "We know the mistress is afraid of the storm, so we have come to stay with you until it is over!"

My cousins and I roamed the mission on our bicycles, climbed the koppie, playing cowboys and Indians, or pretended to be farmers. We got to know the plants and insects there and seemed not to have a care in the world. There is a special kind of smell on South African koppies, and whenever I am in the countryside and get a whiff of it, I am reminded of days spent roaming the Kilnerton koppie.

We would walk up the steep hill to the Kilnerton church on Sundays, breathing in the herby smell, and there I would lose myself in the wonderful singing of the students as they sent up hymns of praise. That little church is now a national monument. Before the advent of Joe into my world, the days at Kilnerton were everything a childhood ought to be.

The sun beats down on my head and shoulders. My hands are as black as the huge lump of coal I am carrying. I'll show those boys. They say that they walked home from school along the railway line yesterday but they could only do it because I was at my music lesson. They say a girl can't manage such a long walk. I'll show them. We must be nearly halfway now and I'm sure they are looking more tired than I am. But I think I am blacker than they are. There are big pieces of coal along the line, and we pick up the biggest pieces we can carry to take home with us.

The Kilnerton station is in sight now and I walk a little faster. I see my mother and Aunt Ethel on the platform. I am scared because I know that the train we should have been on must have got there some time ago.

The police are there with Mom and Aunt Ethel and everyone is cross with us because we have given them such a fright—not being on the train when it pulled into the station. Once we are home and cleaned up, we all get smacked, but Mom comes into the bedroom and dries my tears. I think she is a little proud of me for standing up to the boys. She even says thank you for the lumps of coal we have carried home for the fire. My heart is singing! She approves of what I have done.

CHAPTER FIVE

ALONG COMES JOE

We've just fetched the car from the garage where it has been for repairs. There is a very good mechanic there. Mom says he's good because she never has a problem when he has worked on the car. I am glad, because money is short and the car is a necessity, Mom says.

Today Joe—that is his name—has asked Mom to give him a lift from work. Aunt Ethel is in the car with us. We sit in the back together. We reach the spot where Joe wants to be let out of the car. He leans over and kisses my mother on the lips. I can't breathe. Something about him has made me distrust him from the very beginning. My aunt puts her arm around me and hugs me as she hears me gasp when I see Joe kiss my mother. It is just a peck on the lips, but I can't imagine why he thinks he has the right to do that. I can't imagine why they should kiss each other. What right does the garage mechanic have to kiss the customer? My heart is racing from the shock of it. I really don't like him at all.

I think before she met Joe my mother must have regretted her lonely life and the real concerns that the lack of money and a mate caused her.

To have someone with whom she could share her problems, with whom she could discuss her woes, and possibly as a result find a way out of them, must have seemed to her like the very best the world could offer her right then.

Joe seemed to love and admire her. He thought her beautiful and he pampered her. He paid for things, he shared his winnings when he won on the horses and he didn't expect anyone to make good his losses when they happened. When he lost, we never knew how much. My grandfather used to tease him when he came home from Tattersalls with his pockets empty. "Joe," he would say, "think about the poor bookmaker's children. You have to lose sometimes, otherwise they'll starve!"

Instead, it was my mother who starved—mentally and spiritually. And like the hundreds of women in similar situations before and after her, when he started to beat her, to abuse her physically and emotionally, my mother stayed with him. I realise now that he was also her drinking partner.

My mother was a beautiful woman, with clear skin and dark hair. Her eyes were green—large and expressive—truly the windows to her soul. As the years went by, those windows clouded over and the pain and bewilderment of her life were all that one could see through them.

Before Joe, she had been a spirited and talented woman despite the fact that she drank heavily. I suppose she would be called "quirky" nowadays. My father told tales of how she would spurn offerings of flowers or perfume when he was courting her—and demand tins of asparagus instead. She was a typical "flapper" in the 1920s and rode a motorbike and smoked cheroots. Mom was a very good bridge player and loved the theatre and cinema.

All those things faded and died when Joe came into her life and they began a life in which alcohol played the major role. I look back with sadness at the waste of so much talent and the way a charming and intelligent woman was robbed of happiness.

We are at Kilnerton. The students and my aunt are away on holiday and our lives are in danger for the second time. I wake to a loud banging on the front door. Someone is shouting, "Open the bloody door or I'm going to set fire to this house!" As I struggle to wake from a deep sleep, I hear my mother rushing to the door. I can't believe that she is going to open the door to whatever monster is making this noise and these threats.

It is Joe. He is drunk. As the front door opens, he rushes in and slaps my mother so hard that she falls to the floor. I rush to try and help her up, and he kicks me in the side. I sob from pain and fright. Mom tells me to go back to bed. How can I do that when this drunken bully is attacking us both?

Joe pulls a huge screwdriver from his pocket. It is the biggest screwdriver I have ever seen. Mom has walked to the dining room and puts the table between her and Joe. I rush to her side. He starts to bash the table with the screwdriver, making deep welts in the wood. Slowly he comes around the table towards us and just as slowly we move away. It becomes a kind of dance in slow motion. The three of us move clockwise while the screwdriver beats a slow, threatening rhythm on the table top, a loud, menacing thumping that echoes the wild beating of my heart. Each thump leaves a scar on the table and another on my soul.

The night passes in a blur of fear, but morning comes eventually and Joe leaves the house. My mother sinks into a deep sleep. She was drinking earlier in the evening. I keep waking and listening for Joe's return.

He doesn't return until noon the next day, full of dreadful remorse. He brings my mother a bunch of flowers. I can't understand why she doesn't send him on his way and tell him never to come near us again.

I began to understand when I realised that my mother had also been drunk that night. It was then that it first dawned on me that Mother and Joe were now drinking companions as well as lovers.

My mother began to drink more and more. I watched her closely as she began the downward spiral which was to last the rest of her life. I reached a point where I could tell when she passed from being sober to being inebriated. It was something about her eyes. Only once did I ever mention her drinking to her—or to anyone else, for that matter. Mom was complaining about not having the money to buy some item of my school uniform. I felt as if I was a terrible burden, yet at the back of my mind was the fact that she was able to buy a bottle of brandy every day. I told her so and received an enraged response that sent me back into my silence.

It was around this time that I woke in the early hours of the morning to realise that everything was eerily quiet. I left my bed softly and tiptoed to my mother's room. She wasn't in her bed. With my heart in my mouth I set out to search for her. Walking through the hallway, I noticed that the front door was open. I peeped out into the darkness and spotted my mother sitting on a bench on the veranda. Her eyes were open, but she didn't appear to see or hear anything. When I touched her, she was ice-cold. I took her elbow and lifted her from the bench. She rose and walked with me. I am sure that she didn't know where she was or what she was doing. I had heard the expression "a catatonic state", and it occurred to me that this had to be what was wrong with her.

I got her to her bed and raced to the kitchen to prepare a hot-water bottle. I put it into the bed beside her and then sat by her side, massaging her hands until she started to warm up and appeared to be breathing normally.

I believe that I saved my mother's life that night, yet I never spoke of it to anyone. And never have until now.

I believe she was really afraid of Joe and it was right that she should have been. He had often threatened her life and several times had come very close to taking it. Was there anywhere she could go to escape from him? Would she manage financially? Besides, how would the well-educated daughter of a British gentleman deal with the embarrassment of a drunken, abusive partner, except by hiding it? Especially once she had joined him as a drinking partner.

How many times did she deny any abuse on his part? How many times did she "walk into a door" or "slip on the bath mat"? In the end there must have been occasions when she actually did those things in her drunken state. Joe and my mother were tied together by a shared disease. Leaving Joe was something to put off for as long as possible. In the meantime, her life was wholly taken over by fear. She was afraid of Joe, afraid for her life and, in the end, afraid of losing her job. As successful a teacher as she was, she must have feared that her drinking would catch up with her. Joe's abuse of us continued unabated, and I continued to wonder why my mother stayed around and endured it.

Yet, in the midst of all this there were golden, successful times for my mother, such as when she trained a little choir several years later. She asked her class at the time whether any of them would like to sing in a choir. The children would come to our house to practise and afterwards swarm up the loquat tree in the garden and gorge themselves on the tart yellow fruit, swinging from the branches like so many monkeys, laughing and singing all the while.

When that choir won the premier award at the eisteddfod, the judge wrote, "This choir obviously comes from a very happy studio." Who would have guessed that the "studio" was the living room of an alcoholic, with an upright piano for accompaniment and a loquat tree in the garden?

I think my mother is an example of how alcoholics can get away with their drinking for a long time. She taught generations of pupils in the schools of Pretoria and the rural and farming areas, and is still remembered by them as a kind and very successful teacher. I was, and still am, proud of her.

I loved her deeply and I believe that she loved me. Yet I felt a sense of rejection because her devotion to Joe seemed to surpass any devotion she had for me. The twin devils of alcohol and physical abuse kept her from showing her love for me, and I am sure that she was happier when I was at boarding school, where I was safe and protected from both her drinking and Joe's abuse.

I am grateful that Joe didn't kill either my mother or me, yet I find it hard to believe that we escaped. The continuing abuse and fear of abuse followed us everywhere we went, twenty-four hours a day. During school holidays I would wake up in the night with dread in the pit of my stomach in case I should, at any minute, hear the swearing and the shouting. The thumping of fist upon bone and flesh was enough to make me feel that this man needed to be killed, that he had no right to be living—and living in a place where he was a continual danger to my mother's life and my own.

The terrifying thing was that I was quite sure that it was my fault. My mother kept telling me to stay away when there were scenes and fights. She told me that my presence made things worse and this certainly seemed to be true. I wondered where I belonged. Had my father really not wanted me? Was I the cause of my mother's suffering? With hindsight I realise that Joe was insanely jealous of me and wanted my mother to himself. Yet, when this situation was eventually achieved, he did not stop beating and abusing her.

CHAPTER SIX

BACK TO SCHOOL

Eventually the time came when my mother moved on to another teaching post. We left Kilnerton and I was back at boarding school. I was spared all the turmoil that Joe brought into our lives. I was spared the anticipation of trouble and broken bones, the screaming and swearing. I was spared the intense anxiety night after night about what might happen. Sometimes nothing happened and the evenings were quiet and outwardly happy and relaxed, but there was always the knot in my stomach and the fear of saying something wrong that would trigger an unimaginable outburst.

I was spared this trauma during the school terms, and although I often worried about what might be happening at home, I could lose myself in the routine and safety of the school days. Everything was mapped out for me; certain times for certain things helped me escape into a life where I barely had to think for myself and could just follow the rules. Saturday morning was the time to do our mending and Sunday evening was the time to write letters. Lights out was at a specific time and not much happened to disturb my sleep during the nights in the school dormitory. I had no "responsibilities", such as having to care for my mother, or making sure that we weren't both killed during the night. At school there was nothing to confuse me. I knew exactly what I had to do.

Once again I was in the care of the nuns. The atmosphere was calm and gentle, and I thrived there. I sometimes hear women talk disparagingly of the nuns who taught them in convent schools. Many of them feel that they were encouraged to be prudish and that the subject of sex was ignored as if it did not exist at all.

This was not the case at my school. In fact, most of us even managed to come away from our school days with no sense of embarrassment about our bodies or nudity, although the curtains of our cubicles always had to be securely drawn to ensure complete privacy when we dressed and undressed.

During that time we had a new boarder in our dormitory, with whom I became firm friends. We spent time together during holidays, as she also lived in Pretoria. It never occurred to me to wonder why she was at boarding school although her home, like mine, was quite close to the school. She was also an only child and I thought perhaps that was the reason for sending her to boarding school.

I was shocked to find out many years later that her mother had also been an alcoholic. There we were, two suffering young girls, and we never told anyone about our circumstances at home. It is much safer to try to ignore the facts and to behave in such a way that people will believe that you are like everyone else—or the way they believe everyone else should be.

I had started taking piano lessons while we were living at Kilnerton. Playing the piano and learning to sing were two of the most important things in my life at the time. I found peace and contentment in being able to make music, and that has stayed with me all my life.

My music teacher was Dr Anna Marsh, who was the first female doctor of music in South Africa. She was a short, plump, dark-haired woman, who showed me such love and caring that I was devoted to her from the start.

When I took music examinations, Dr Marsh would appear in my dormitory to make sure that I was up in time and ready for the exam. She was always with me in the waiting room beforehand. In winter she brought a hot-water bottle with a knitted cover—it was blue with pink embroidered roses—and made me hold my hands under the cover to make sure that my fingers were warm and supple when I had to enter the exam room.

I had seldom been nurtured in this way, and Dr Anna Marsh remains forever in my memory as someone who took a loving interest in me and in what I could achieve.

CHAPTER SEVEN

GRANDPA—AND JOE, OF COURSE

My grandparents used to stay with each of their three daughters for about four months of the year—or however long it suited everyone.

I remember a time when Granny and Grandpa were staying with my mother. We rented a large house in Pretoria, and two rooms were set aside for them. Joe lived in a cottage in the garden.

Packing my trunk to go back to school always raised mixed feelings in me. I was glad to return to the calm, gentle atmosphere of the school, but always worried about what might be happening at home.

I look down at the piles of clothes on my bed. It is time to go back to school for the winter term. I need to check that everything is here. I count the number of vests, shirts, pants and stockings piled neatly near the pillow and then turn around to make sure of the gymslips. Grandpa comes into the room and hands me a parcel. "What is this, Grandpa?" I ask.

"For you, my girl." And with that he turns and walks out of the room.

I look inside and find a brand-new school blazer. Just yesterday Grandpa stopped by me as I sat eating my breakfast and fingered the rather threadbare cardigan I was wearing. "Is this all you have to keep you warm at school, my child?" he asked.

"Yes, Grandpa," I replied, "but it's okay."

I believe that a close, loving and supportive family is beyond price. I had a close and warm relationship with my grandparents and with my mother's two sisters and their children. I can remember joyful holidays spent with my cousins and Christmases filled with warmth and laughter.

Granny and Grandpa were an important source of stability in my life: a devoted pair, who had taught together at a farm school in the early days of their marriage. They continued to teach throughout their lives.

My grandfather came to South Africa during the second Boer War. He was in the Cameron Highlanders. The country—and, I suspect, my granny—made such an impression on him that he stayed for the rest of his life.

Grandpa was a gentleman of the old school: kind, courteous and able to mix with all kinds of people without causing embarrassment either to them or to himself. It was only after his death that I realised that this gentle man, so beloved by his pupils over the years, a man who had meant the world to his family because of his devotion and care, had also had a background of courage and pain, which had taken him through the Egyptian campaign as well as the Boer War and the First World War.

He had two "skills" that made him special to me as a child. He could draw seashells with consummate skill and he invented an aunt for my cousins and me. She was called Aunt Regina and her surname was spelled Ffoulkes-Fothergill but pronounced Forgie-Fiske! Aunt Regina had lived for years in China and could recite "Chinese nursery rhymes". The one that lives in my memory goes like this:

> *Was gal Mairlee hadee lammee*
> *Fleecee allee samee likee wool*
> *Ebrywhere dat Mairlee gal walkee*
> *Baba hoppee long too.*

These rhymes sent all the cousins into gales of helpless laughter.

My grandpa was the man of the family for me. He was always there with his gentle, loving smile. He told my cousins and me stories and teased us unmercifully. He was always willing to listen to us and liked to know how we were doing at school.

I didn't know it then, but I know now that my grandparents and my aunts, and even my father's brother and sister, all contributed towards the cost of keeping me at that expensive school, where I would be protected, at least during term time, from Joe's drunken violence and my mother's alcoholism.

Late one night there was a shattering of glass, a roar of rage, and I knew immediately what was happening. Leaping out of bed with not much idea of what I could do, I found Joe, his thin, cruel lips drawn back, holding my mother by the throat. The police had taken him away earlier, but at four o'clock in the morning he was back. He had broken down the front door and was taking out his rage on my mother.

Joe's antics had woken my grandparents at two in the morning. Grandpa had immediately called the police, and when they had arrived it had taken two of them to grab hold of Joe and take him to their van.

Although he was quite short, Joe was a wiry beast. Strong and enraged, he had flung one of the policemen off the veranda into the flower bed below. The policeman's helmet had flown right off his head and rolled onto the pathway.

Eventually they had got him to their van but obviously they had just kept him there until they had finished their rounds and arrived back at the station. Then they had let him go.

Here he was, breaking down our front door, still drunk, two hours later. My grandfather appeared in the doorway and Joe released my mother and made a move towards Grandpa. I was terrified as I watched him threaten my grandfather. I knew I was quite capable of stabbing Joe to death with a kitchen knife should he lay a finger on the old man.

But that old man seemed fearless, and the look in his eye told Joe that if he tried anything he would do so at his peril. Joe broke down into yet another fit of remorse and promised that it would never happen again.

It is Easter. I have just celebrated my eleventh birthday at school, surrounded by warmth and love. I go home alone on Easter Monday. It is impossible for me to invite friends home for the day or for the holidays, because I never know when there will be a drunken scene from Joe, and I have noticed that my mother is starting to drink more and more.

It is just as well that I haven't brought a friend home with me this Easter Monday because Joe is angry that I have come home. He would rather have me stay at school and so he tears up all my clothes. He shouts as he rips up every stitch I own. His face is contorted and red. His thin lips are pulled back from his teeth, which show white in a parody of a grin.

I don't have many clothes. Money in our household is spent on brandy before clothes, so it is a big loss for me. Even my underclothes aren't spared. As he finishes demolishing one garment, he furiously attacks the next until there is nothing left but strips fit only for the bag that holds the dusting and polishing rags.

I go back to school in a fog that night. It is one of the very few times that I experience real homesickness and I burst into tears at the supper table. The sister in charge of the refectory puts her arm around me and takes me out into the corridor. I am too embarrassed and ashamed to tell her what happened at home. I say that I am homesick. I don't know how much the sisters know about my circumstances. Gently she leads me to the phone in the office and tells me to phone home. I dial the number and am comforted to hear my mother talking quite normally, sounding sober, and reassuring me that she loves me.

She tells me that my one of my aunts is already at her sewing machine, making me some new dresses and that the other is going to buy me some underclothes. I hope she will buy me some pretty new petticoats.

Nothing will ever erase the memory of that awful Easter Monday, but I do remember happy times. Though I was mostly a lonely, frightened child, the love of my family was important and comforting to me. I remember the days of the old cinemas. There was a "fire curtain" between the audience and the screen. It was always painted with colourful scenes, usually birds and creepers and exotic flowers. It was there for the audience to look at while they were waiting for the film to begin. Just before the lights went down, it would slowly rise and disappear into the ceiling. I made a fire curtain for myself, with happy pictures on the front to show the world.

To this day, I have my fire curtain. I bring it down between myself and the "audience". I show them pretty pictures. I keep it lowered in front of me to protect myself from being hurt. No, that's not true. I bring it down so that people can't see if I am hurt.

CHAPTER EIGHT

EASTER AND CHRISTMAS

Easter was a very important and a very happy time for me at school. Because we had three terms a year (compared with the government schools, which had four) we did not have school holidays at Easter time, but it was no hardship to stay at school over Easter.

I can feel the cold air around my knees. I try to remain motionless as I kneel. This is such an important thing that I am doing, keeping watch over the Host in the chapel on Maundy Thursday night. There was a Mass, at which the bread and wine was blessed before it was moved to the Chapel of Repose, where it is now and will stay until Good Friday night. I enjoyed the singing in the chapel as we sang the rather sad hymns. Now that the Host is in the chapel we take it in turns to keep watch all night.

I wish I could rest my behind against the pew behind me, but the pews are not bolted to the floor and will slide noisily backwards if any behinds should lean against them. My back aches as I kneel in an upright position. The teachers tell us that kneeling in chapel is a good way to develop strong back muscles, and that is very important for young girls. I suppose it also helps me to get a Good Deportment badge every year.

The chill is getting into my bones; the breeze is around my face and head as well as my knees. I struggle to keep a straight back while I make sure that my hands are folded in front of my face.

It is so quiet. I think I can feel the presence of the God that the sisters talk about.

I smell the incense and the sweet perfume of the white St Joseph's lilies in front of the altar. I can hear the other girls in the chapel moving, trying to ease their limbs. I take a peep and see their silhouettes, their veils stirring slightly in the breeze. The silence is eerie.

I wonder if God will send me some sign to let me know that I am loved and that Joe has not been sent to punish me for sins that I don't think I know about.

There were no sounds on Good Friday, except the scrape of children's feet on the old stone floors, or coughs and sneezes, interrupted by the sound of pages turning as we read only religious literature. The story of the Crucifixion is a scary one for children. Hammering nails into human flesh is not something that they hear without being appalled. I remember reading the story in the Bible at about the age of eight and crying inconsolably while doing so.

Boredom had us yawning and fidgeting as we observed a twenty-four hour silence through the day. Every year someone would get the giggles, and this would spread through the ranks like a veld fire out of control. Girls would scatter in all directions, handkerchiefs to their faces, eyes watering, trying to control not just their laughter but often their bladders too. There were always some whose giggling fits made them wet their pants.

The very young children were taken out into the street for a walk every hour. Little kids in brown uniforms walked in a "crocodile", two by two, around the suburb, trying hard not to hop and skip for joy at being released into the world outside.

Jacquie, Stella and I take an old black portable wind-up gramophone down to the spot we think is furthest from the school buildings. We conceal it under a blanket in the hope that anyone seeing us will think that we are bound for a peaceful spot in the jacaranda walk where we can read our religious books undisturbed. But the real purpose of the blanket is to put it over the gramophone to muffle the sound. We lie on our tummies with our heads under the blanket so that we can hear the music. We don't have one of those gadgets to sharpen the needles—and no money to buy new ones—so the music is tinny. It doesn't matter to us because the fun is really in the way we are breaking the Good Friday rules. I doze off.

I am woken by someone pulling at my legs and dragging me out from under the blanket. Jacquie and Stella are also sticking their heads out into the air.

Bust! There is a prefect whose wrath shows in the frown she is wearing.

"You realise you have broken the rules in the worst possible way, don't you?" she whispers, breaking her silence for the day.

We hang our heads and look—and feel—sheepish.

"I'm going to have to report you, you know?" she says, as she rips the blanket off the gramophone. Suddenly Frank Sinatra's very special crooning surrounds us and we rush to lift the needle before anyone hears it. The prefect bursts out laughing.

"Oh, go on then," she says, trying hard to control her giggles. "But you'll have to give me that record, or I'll report you."

We rip the record from the turntable, thrust it into her hands and run for our lives.

The choir is singing the hymn "Jesus Christ is Risen Today". I love this hymn. It is tuneful and triumphant. The chapel is beautiful and Easter Sunday makes it seem even more beautiful than usual. St Joseph's lilies tumble from urns in front of the altar and the paschal candle, fat and solid, burns brightly to one side.

When I was eight, I was one of the servers, called the "boat boy", and it was my job to hold the vessel in which the incense was kept, opening it when the priest needed to refill the censer before he held it up and swung it back and forth to distribute the sharp perfume through the chapel.

I have grown too big to be a boat boy, but I am happy to have graduated to the choir. The singing at school is always beautiful and, although there are no boys' voices to join us, we sing in three parts: soprano, contralto and descant. Being in the choir makes me feel secure and respected, an important part of the school.

The rest of Easter Sunday is a riot of Easter egg hunts and a huge iced cake for tea. The younger girls sit at the head of the tables while the seniors and the prefects wait on them. Gales of laughter fill the large room and the sense of celebration fills our hearts. Easter is a weekend full of the smell of incense from the chapel, the smell of moss from the Easter gardens and the enticing aroma of the chocolate eggs.

The weekend ends warmly and wonderfully, with Sister Superior reading to us from *The House at Pooh Corner*, and I always wait for her to make a mistake and say, "Hell, Hell a horrible heffalump". What a terrible thing that would be to happen to a nun! We are all half asleep at the end of an exciting day, but waiting and hoping for this terrible faux pas keeps me awake.

One Easter we had a big surprise at school. We were given a four-month-old donkey. I believe that the idea had been to name the donkey Brother Jonathan, but we ended up having to call her Jenny. Jenny was no docile, timid, gentle donkey. She was an ever-present source of exasperation, interest and diversion. She ate the flowers in the garden, trampled the beds and brayed loudly at all the wrong times.

I delighted in the advent of Jenny in the life of the school. I had never had pets at home. We once had a puppy, but Joe treated it so abominably that my mother gave it away to a family that would care for it. So Jenny became my pet, and I would often creep away from the other girls to feed her an apple that I had managed to squirrel away from the breakfast table, or to give her a bit of a brush in the time that I had available.

The following entry appears in the book to mark the centenary of the school: "Jenny had no particular role at the school unless it was in the famous school Nativity play, when she carried Mary through the grounds on her journey to Bethlehem. It took a few years before she could be trusted with the task, but she eventually undertook it. She was led out for her first rehearsal. Jenny was no fool and took in the situation at a glance. She quickly took over from the senior girl who was leading her onto the terrace and started to dance up and down, pirouetting and prancing, scattering a bevy of cherubs.

"But Jenny did eventually take her solemn role in the play seriously and was one of the stars of the show. In the months from one Nativity play to the next, she was harnessed to a little cart and helped the gardeners."

The school presented the Nativity play every December towards the end of the last school term of the year. The play was a very important event in the life of the school. All of us looked forward to it, and most girls wanted a part in it. It was a very important part of my life too.

The first time that I had an important part in the Nativity play I was about six years old. I nearly fell over as I stood on my orange. I felt the wetness from the pulp as the orange burst. I wanted to giggle. Ruth was dancing opposite me. A few moments ago we had been playing with the orange as if it were a ball. In previous years I had been one of the shepherds, but this year Ruth and I were guests at the inn in Bethlehem where there was no room for Mary and Joseph and the baby Jesus.

I started to giggle and wondered if anyone had noticed that my orange was flat and messy. I could see that Ruth was giggling too. I didn't know whether to leave the orange where it was or to pick it up and throw it into the flower beds at the edge of the terrace. I supposed I had better do that, or someone else might tread on it and, as we were all barefoot, it would make a mess of someone else's feet as well.

The joy I had in taking part in the Nativity play has stayed with me through all the years since I left school. It was part of my Christmas celebrations. The celebrations at home were not always joyful.

The Nativity play had the status of a service, a form of worship. It was presented on the front terraces of the school, with the audience on the highest terrace, while the play was being performed on the lower one. The choir sang from a first floor balcony overlooking the terrace. It formed an eyrie above the terrace, where the singers could see the players but the audience could not see them. When I joined the choir at the age of eleven, I liked to think that our voices were sweet and true as they rang out into the evening, like hidden angels come to join the gathering.

The costumes were to be wondered at. No large safety pins crudely attached wings to angels' backs. The wings were large and beautiful and looked real enough to help any angel fly. And no striped towels were to be found on the heads of shepherds as they watched over their sheep in the fields by night. Proper headdresses in colourful material were used for the shepherds as well as the guests at the inn. The innkeeper and his wife were appropriately dressed, and all the costumes were carefully stored, mended and cared for from one December to the next.

These memories of Easter and Christmas and the part they played in the life of the school are very important to me for the contribution they have made to my view of the world. I remember those plays quite vividly. I am afraid to go back to see one today, in case they have changed so much that the very special part they played in my life at school is ruined.

CHAPTER NINE

A NEW FAMILY

After my parents' divorce I saw my father on a fairly regular basis. He would visit me at school or sometimes take me out on Sundays. We would go to visit his brother and sister, who lived quite close to the school. Neither of them was married, and they both showered love and attention on me.

In all that time I never said anything to my father about what was happening to my mother and how Joe was affecting our lives. I realise today that he knew that my mother was drinking. After all, hadn't he accused her of this before the divorce? Yet he never asked me about it, nor did he, to my knowledge, make any attempt to find out whether she was still drinking and, if so, how it was affecting my life.

Just before the end of the war my father married again. I am not sure what year it was.

The first time I set eyes on my stepmother I am eleven years old. The dining table is perched right on the edge of a gaping hole in the floor. I don't know why it is there, and it frightens me: a big, black hole, the kind one reads about in stories, the kind that is used by wicked stepmothers to torture their stepchildren. They put the kids down holes like that to spend terrifying days in the dark.

My father tells me that the floor has been eaten away by white ants and that the workmen are due the next day to mend the floor and close up the hole.

We are sitting at dinner, just the three of us: my father, my new stepmother and I. I am anxious and self-conscious. I feel I am being put to the test. What does she think of me? I know that I'm not a baby any more and it is silly to be afraid of the hole in the floor, but I can't help feeling that maybe I will end up at the bottom of it.

The rain is drumming down on the corrugated iron roof, with a crashing sound so loud that you can hear nothing else. Thunder bellows, lightning flashes, and no one tries to talk. There are no curtains at the windows.

As the storm dies away, I am intensely conscious of the embarrassment we are all feeling. Dad tries a few jokes, and we giggle nervously. I start to hum to myself to hide my embarrassment. My father rounds on me furiously, "Jean! We don't sing at table."

I flush and tears spring to my eyes. I lower my eyes to my plate, determined not to let them fall. Dad sees the flush and the tears and reaches across and puts his hand on my arm. "It's okay, my love," he says. "We love you."

I know he wants to reassure me, but his words and actions don't relieve the embarrassment and hurt I feel at being so sharply corrected by my father in front of this rather intimidating woman. She is someone else I need to please to keep my place in the family.

My mother blamed this woman for the break-up of her marriage and had painted me a picture of someone ruthless, out to get what she wanted. She had told me that my father didn't want me any more, and so I entered his new household and met his new wife, Evelyn, with a strong sense of not belonging or being wanted there.

After the first disastrous dinner Evelyn didn't look so bad to me. She had the kindest blue eyes I had ever seen, and I felt drawn to her.

As we spent more time together on my visits to my father, we became friends, and I came to trust her. However, it wasn't until I grew to be an adult that I became close to her and began to understand the difficulties that she must have experienced, allowing a young child into her home during the first days of her marriage. Evelyn accepted me and approved of me. She never made me feel that I was an intruder in her home or that she resented my presence there.

I remember times spent with her in the town where she and my father lived. Dad was out all day, trying to get a new business established, while I spent the time with Evelyn and her new baby son, Daniel.

The advent of my half-brother was a highlight in my life. I was no longer an only child.

The times that I stayed in my father's home were the closest I came to being with a normal family. Evelyn kept a strict routine, and I was allowed to push the pram each afternoon as we took the baby for a walk, laughing at the loud, somewhat unfortunate colours of some of the neighbouring houses and enjoying the sunshine and fresh air.

A few years later my younger sister was born, a sweet-smelling bundle of blonde and blue, and I loved her as much as I loved my little brother.

There was a spell during which Dad and Evelyn rented a small farm outside a sleepy town in the Transvaal. I enjoyed going there. I was allowed to dress my baby sister and play with my brother. Evelyn treated me like an adult, and we would drink tea together in the afternoons, sitting in the shade of a thorn tree in the back garden. These were quiet times when I felt accepted and loved.

I find it difficult to recollect the exact time of my visits with my father and Evelyn. Yet I recall the incidents quite clearly.

My father had his head in his hands and was sobbing. I couldn't believe that this was happening, and it broke my heart to see him so distressed. I'd never seen him cry before. We were sitting at the supper table: just Evelyn, Dad and me.

I had no idea what could have reduced him to such a state. I was too young to realise that he might well have been worried about my mother's drinking and what might be happening to me at home. I have wondered since if that had been the case. Did he find it too difficult to talk to me about it? To ask me what my life was like when I wasn't with him? Did he fear that he may have to take me to live with him? I don't think that Evelyn would for one moment have baulked at the idea.

The family was short of money and struggled to make ends meet. Would having me join them have stretched the budget to breaking point? Certainly taking a child who is twelve years older than her half-brother into a fairly new marriage would have been quite an undertaking.

"Elizabeth phoned to say that Jean has a dental appointment that she has forgotten about and she must go home tomorrow morning," he said. I was appalled. I knew of no such appointment and I was sure that my mother had made it up so that I wouldn't be able to spend a full two weeks with my dad.

My father left the table and Evelyn followed him, leaving me on my own, unable to touch my food and wondering where this turn of events was going to lead me.

I adored my mother and found it quite impossible to face up to what was happening to her and to me. She was drinking heavily and Joe was beating us regularly. I was tempted, that night of my father's tears, to tell him about it. Yet it seemed disloyal to my mother. Being an only child is rough. Circumstances such as those into which I was thrust led me to withdraw even more from those around me. I seemed to have no one whom I could really trust, and so I cradled all the terrors of my life in my own heart and mind and never learned to share them with anyone. I desperately wanted peace between my parents, but my mother found it impossible to let go, while my father was trying to build a new life for himself and his new family.

The next morning my father drove me home. There was, of course, no dental appointment and my mother tried to make light of it, saying that she had made a mistake.

When I was about fourteen, my father had a series of heart attacks. The only way heart attacks were treated in those days was by weeks of bed rest. So began the deterioration of his life and the lives of his wife and two young children. Without his dedication and the hard work it had taken to establish his business, it failed and poverty became a reality for the family.

Evelyn took a teaching job to put food on the table and to pay the rent. Nevertheless, I was always welcome, no matter how poor the circumstances.

For my fourteenth birthday I remember Evelyn giving me a pretty blue vase that she had made some years before. At the time I thought it a rather inappropriate gift for a teenager and had no idea of the sadness she must have experienced at having no money at all to buy even a small gift for me. She had made a real sacrifice by giving me one of her treasures, and I wasn't able to appreciate it until many years later.

Not long after this my father seemed to have recovered some strength, and he and Evelyn moved to Uitenhage in the Eastern Cape, where my father had managed to obtain a job.

I seldom saw them in the next few years, but Evelyn wrote to me regularly and a caring correspondence began between us. This helped me to understand that my father loved me and regarded me as an important member of his family. So did Evelyn.

CHAPTER TEN

THE FIRST DRINK

Joe's abuse continued and I still felt that I was to blame.

One terrifying night he chased us with the same axe that lay beside the fireplace, and we fled into the street and along the pavement in an attempt to escape. Heart pounding and fear clasping at my guts, I held on to my mother's arm and steered her along the concrete path. Joe, very drunk, jumped into his car and followed us, intent on running us down. I saw him try to mount the pavement. I dragged my mother, who was also drunk, along with me. I opened a gate and ran up to a front door. I rang the doorbell with all my might. As the door opened, I could see beyond the woman who was standing there. There was a warm fire and a smiling family gathered in the front room.

I wanted to ask her to help us, but she took one look at us and shouted, "They're drunk!' and slammed the door in our faces.

I was only fifteen, but I was already aware that most doors were closed to people like us.

My anxiety about being abandoned never left me during all that time. My mother and I spent one Christmas holiday in Durban. We stayed at a beachfront hotel. I think my grandparents paid for it.

One evening my mom was asked to go out with some of the other residents. I was left behind, perfectly safe and well looked after for my evening meal in the hotel and able to join in some of the activities that were laid on for the young people.

I was so anxious and afraid about whether or not my mother would return, that I couldn't bring myself to participate in the games. I went to our room instead, where I read my book, waiting for my mother's return. The hours ticked by and I became more and more concerned about whether she would come back to me. I knew that she would be drinking. I convinced myself that she might be involved in an accident and no one would know that I even existed. I'm not sure any more whether I really believed that she would abandon me, but I do know that the threat of being left alone in the world was very real to me that night.

Later I had reached such a state of anxiety that I vomited into the hand basin in the hotel room. I was too afraid to go out of the room and down the corridor to the toilets to be sick there.

Of course the plughole in the hand basin became clogged. When my mother did arrive home in the early hours, she found me desperately trying to clear the basin. She was very angry and shouted at me for being such a baby and for not going to the toilet if I was feeling sick. I suspect that her anger was related to the fact that she had been drinking and perhaps felt guilt and remorse for having left me for so long.

She didn't know about my fear of abandonment, and I was too afraid to let her know just how much of a baby I was.

I like to think that if she had known about my fear, she might have put her arms around me and reassured me that she would never abandon me.

My sixteenth birthday is on a Sunday and the entire family is there. It is a day for family. There is a lot of love in the room. We are going to have a big Sunday dinner to celebrate. Mom has prepared a roast and my favourite baked custard pudding. All the cousins are here, and Granny and Grandpa too. I am standing at the edge of the room, watching. The room is filled with laughter and teasing, shining faces and jokes. Yet I feel as if I am standing on the edge of it all. I don't feel good enough to join in.

The table is laid: knives and forks set out correctly, facing in the right direction, each piece carefully placed in accordance with the rules of etiquette. My maternal great-grandmother used to be "in service" in Arundel Castle in England, and so we have all been taught the correct way of laying a table. The cutlery is silver-plated, not silver, but it has been polished and it glistens as the sun shines into the room, making it warm and pleasant on this autumn afternoon. Why doesn't it warm me too? What is it about me that makes me different? Why can't I just fit in like everyone else seems to? My heart aches, and I wish that I could just slink away to my bedroom and lose myself in a book.

Mom comes up and puts her arm around me. "Come on, love," she says. "Have just a little glass of sherry. It will make you feel good and it won't do you any harm." She knows quite well that I frown on drinking and have vowed never to drink.

I don't want to end up like my mother, a drunk tied to another drunk, abused and ashamed.

But perhaps one little glass of sherry won't do me any harm? I succumb and sip at just a tiny glassful.

It's magic. I feel warm inside, prettier than I have ever thought I could be, good enough to join the rest of the family, to joke and laugh. I feel so good I need another glass of sherry to keep the feeling going and so I creep into the pantry to pour myself another secret glass of sherry.

The next thing I know it is about eight o'clock at night. I smell of vomit, my head aches and I can't remember how I got to my bed. Didn't I have a date to go to friends with my boyfriend, Robert, that night? Mom tells me that she phoned him to tell him that I was ill.

After dinner I apparently crept back to the pantry and "kept the feeling going" by having another glass of sherry and then another. Glass by little sherry glass I finished that bottle. I must have smelled strongly of sherry and it must have been obvious that I was drunk.

But no one said anything about it. No one asked me any questions. What I did that night is typical of the way an alcoholic drinks. Once I started, I found that I couldn't stop.

It is frightening that most people are ignorant about alcoholism. Taking drugs is against the law. Drinking alcohol is not only socially acceptable but also expected of one. I don't approve of or subscribe to temperance societies, or those who advocate them. There are many people who can drink with impunity, who enjoy the taste and the sociability of having a drink. They never get into trouble through their drinking. I believe that if one's drinking is getting one into trouble, there is a need to take a long hard look at one's drinking habits.

I was in my matric year and I was certainly in trouble that night of my sixteenth birthday. How frightening it is that no steps were taken to talk to me about what had happened. Did my mother shirk this responsibility because of her own drinking? I don't think so. I think that alcoholism was not something one talked about in the late 1940s. I can, however, remember my mother and Joe making a joke about Alcoholics Anonymous, laughing about it and saying that they would never consider joining, as if it would be a huge comedown for them to be seen there. There was no admission from them that either of them had a drinking problem.

I learned later that Alcoholics Anonymous started in South Africa in 1946, so it was new and not much was probably known about the organisation at the time.

CHAPTER ELEVEN

NEW BEGINNINGS

It is the end of the year and my days in the safe haven of school are coming to an end.

It is several years after my beloved Jenny the donkey arrived at the school. I am kneeling on the damp grass. I feel the gentle breeze and see the stars, sense the anticipation of the audience as I raise my arms heavenward in the last Nativity play of my school years. I hear my own voice ring out as that of the angel Gabriel, "O Adonai! In the beginning was the Word and the Word was with God and the Word was God. And without Him was not anything made that was made." It rained earlier in the afternoon and the air is still fresh and cool. I can smell the wet earth and feel the damp beneath my knees as I kneel on the lawn and speak the opening lines of the play.

Jenny behaves perfectly too, plodding around the rose garden with a blue-veiled Mary sitting demurely on her back.

I watch with a sense of sadness and loss as the procession of the Kings weaves its way along the jacaranda walk and through the rose garden, burning torches held aloft by little pages to light their way. I feel anxious about my future. This is my last Nativity play, my last year in the safety of the school that has been my home for twelve years.

So much water has gone under the bridge between the time I squashed my orange and tonight, when I am playing the part of the angel Gabriel. I am sixteen years old. It has always been my ambition to play the part of Gabriel. Most other girls long for the part of Mary.

Gabriel starts the Nativity play, rising from a spotlight that illuminates the darkness where the circle of archangels kneels, to shout his stunning announcement to the waiting world.

I couldn't have been given a better farewell gift from the school.

Shortly after I had left school, Joe took a job in the Eastern Transvaal. He phoned my mother often and I soon realised that he was keen for her to join him. She came to me one evening and told me that she had decided to marry him.

I was appalled. I couldn't believe my ears. I could think of no good reason for her to have made that decision. I still can't. My mother's decision to marry Joe remains one of the great mysteries of my life, and I will never understand it.

The times that I had spent with my father on holiday were serene and loving, and he had made it clear that I would be welcome to become part of his family again. His response to my letter asking him if I could come to live near him was excited and positive.

I sat on the train and I couldn't stop weeping. I vaguely remembered a little verse that my mother had taught me during earlier train journeys.

"I think I can, I think I can, I think I can . . ." went the words in time to the chuffing of the train. As the train picks up speed, the words change to "I'm doing it, I'm doing it, I'm doing it . . ." and eventually the engine gets into its stride and the refrain becomes "It's easy, it's easy, it's easy . . ."

But it wasn't easy. Big changes in one's life never are.

I moved in with my father's family, close-knit and set in their ways. Fitting in is never easy, and at the age of seventeen, withdrawn and anxious, it was very hard for me.

There was no bedroom for me in the house where Dad and Evelyn were living at the time and so they hired a room for me in the neighbour's garden. As old as I was, I was terrified to be alone in that room. It had no lavatory and I had to go outside and through a gate to use the one leading off the back stoep of our house. What terrifying journeys in the dark those were.

I am still afraid of the dark and of being out of doors alone at night. I certainly no longer believe in ghosts or fear that I will be abandoned, so I suspect that my fears have developed out of habit.

Years after Joe had died, I discovered among his possessions a letter that my mother had written, telling him that I had gone to live with my father and that she was now prepared to marry him. Joe had scrawled across the envelope, "Jean has been pushed off and everything is rosy." How pleased he must have been to be rid of me. I sometimes wonder if my mother was too. I know that the discovery of that letter cut me to the quick.

CHAPTER TWELVE

THE LAWYER

When people had asked me what I wanted to do when I left school, I had always answered that I wanted to be a lawyer. However, all my efforts to find a lawyer under whose supervision I could do my articles had been in vain. They didn't want girls in those days. Dad told me that he thought he had found one in the little town in which he lived, who might be willing to take me on. I would need to serve five years of legal articles, study by correspondence and write the attorneys' admission exam.

I sit in the small, untidy waiting room, waiting for the lawyer to appear. Electric lights without shades hang from the ceilings. I expect to see men with green eyeshades, sitting on tall stools and writing in large books with quill pens.

I read too much Dickens.

Looking around, I find that the place is a hive of activity. Two typists peck away at their typewriters, which clack and tremble at the pace. The young woman behind the counter is talking rudely to the thin, poorly dressed coloured woman who is making a payment on her debt.

Mr Levin, old Max, as I later came to think of him, is a surprise: tall and gangly, almost completely bald, with a Shylock nose and a twinkle in his eye. He has a harelip, which causes him to shower everything around him with a fine spray of saliva.

"I really am in two minds about taking you on as an articled clerk," he says. "You must know yourself that you won't finish your articles. A woman is meant to get married and have babies and five years is going to be a long time for you to stay in an office with your nose to the grindstone."

I am at a loss for words—and very angry too.

"You are a pretty girl," he goes on. "You're not going to last the course." I am not just at a loss for words. I am dumbstruck.

I want to punch him on the nose. What does he know about what girls can or can't do and what right does he have to refuse to take me on because I am a girl? I grab my handbag and start to rise from my chair.

However, as I do so, he puts out a hand to stop me.

"I have a soft spot for your father," he says, "so I will sign you on as an articled clerk, but you must learn shorthand and typing first. When you bring me your certificate, I will sign the papers."

I feel somewhat taken aback, but tell him that I will do it. I need to prove that I am worthy of this.

Old Max immediately produces the name, address and phone number of a suitable teacher.

After four weeks of intensive typing and shorthand study I presented myself at the offices opposite the magistrates' court with a shorthand and typing diploma clutched in my hand.

An articled clerk in an attorney's office is not someone who has any privileges or status. My job was to run errands for the attorneys, to keep the debt record cards up to date in the debt collection department and to dash back and forth across the road to the clerk of the court's office to get legal documents stamped and processed!

I felt myself to be an object of scorn there. The still pimply young male clerks glanced at me from the corners of their eyes, and it was quite clear that they thought I had a damned cheek thinking that I, a girl, could ever become an attorney.

However, I soon found that being a "mere girl" had its advantages. Old Max was so proud of the fact that he had done something as extraordinary as taking on a female clerk that he was determined to make sure that I studied and learned everything that I would need to get me through the exam at the end of the year. It was not common for articled clerks to pass their exam the first time they wrote it.

There is high tension all around me. The court is packed with spectators. It is not often that we have a murder trial in this one-horse town. My heart is beating fast. The man in the dock is trembling, his face grey with fear. He has just been found guilty.

My mind slides back to the day that he came into the office across the road. He was looking for someone to defend him on a charge of murder. The body of a man had been found in the boot of a car parked at the railway station. The car had a Grahamstown registration plate. The police had done good work to track down the man who, they believed, was responsible for the murder. But where had the murder taken place? If the victim had been killed in Grahamstown then the trial of the suspect should take place there. If he had been killed in our town, then the trial would need to be held there when next the circuit court came around.

I am drawn from my reverie into the present. This is the circuit court. Much of the defence case has been based on the long hours of work that I put in looking through decided cases, scrutinising legal tomes for references and information that could be useful to our counsel. I have been present at every meeting with old Max and counsel. How much I have learned through those days, and some nights too!

Every day I have been sitting in one of the front rows reserved for the public, with my headscarf on. I listened to every bit of evidence led. Now the guilty verdict has been given and I know that the judge is going to sentence the man to death. I become aware of him glaring sternly at me as he reaches for the black cap I know he will put on his head before he pronounces the death penalty. As if in a dream I see him point at me as he says, "You, young lady, please leave this court room." I can't believe my ears. In answer to my look of disbelief he continues, "You are too young to be sitting here watching this."

How angry I am! Old enough to help to prepare the case but not to be present at its ending!

On Wednesday afternoons when the offices were closed, old Max used to make me bring my lecture notes and textbooks and we would sit in the dusty, half dark offices, surrounded by great heaps of files—tied together with pink tape—and he would go through them with me, explaining and questioning and putting me to the test. Those afternoons were very different from the afternoons of the rest of the week. No hubbub of phones, voices or the arguments and tears of couples embarking on the road to the divorce court. Old Max himself would add to the general noise and feverish activity when he lost his temper and swore loudly at his brother and partner. His colourful swearwords never failed to bring all the eyes in the waiting room up and out of the ancient magazines and cause them to be fixed on the door to old Max's office.

But on Wednesday afternoons there was absolute quiet, and the blinds were down to shut out the world. The phones were silent, and we sat, just the two of us, in the gloom and the smell of dust, while the wise old man tried to help this young girl to absorb and understand the intricacies of Roman Dutch Law. It seemed to me that the smell of dust was in those textbooks rather than in the pink-beribboned files around us.

At the end of my first year of articles old Max grabs me by the hand and drags me from my desk. "Come on," he yells. "The exam results are out!" I can hear my heart thumping in my chest and adrenaline levels are high as we run to the post office. He is shouting (and spitting) as we run. I gather that he has arranged for the post office to keep my post rather than deliver it to my home later. But all I can think of is what if I have failed after all the time he has given up for me? I remind him that if there is a green slip in the results envelope, it means I have passed, but if the slip is pink, then I have failed.

The man behind the counter hands the envelope to old Max, who passes it to me. My fingers are stiff, and I can hear my heart beat loudly in my ears. I tear open the envelope.

It is green! Old Max catches me up in his arms and swings me around, shouting with glee. Passers-by must think we're mad, and some even stop to stare at us. Old Max is mayor of the town and very well known. God knows what they think is going on today.

I am stunned. How did I, from behind my curtain, achieve something like this?

Old Max tells me that I am let off all work for the rest of the day, but first he insists on escorting me to all the attorneys' offices in the village so that he can gloat about his female articled clerk.

It turns out not to be such fun, however, because we find that all the other articled clerks (men only) have failed. I can't really be gleeful in these circumstances, though I admit to feeling just a little cock-a-hoop.

CHAPTER THIRTEEN

FALLING IN LOVE

My father looks at me with a twinkle in his eye and says, "Now, that's just the kind of chap I would like you to marry."

"Good heavens, Dad, don't try to make me a match. I'll make my own choice, thank you very much." He's talking about the chairman of the United Party Youth in the town, a slender man of average height with very black curly hair, a big nose and a prominent Adam's apple. What I mainly notice, though, are his large deep blue eyes that shine with laughter and crease at the corners when he smiles at me. We're at a fundraising dance and everyone is here—it's quite a social event. Earlier I had been chatting to a new acquaintance when I heard a whispered conversation behind me. "That's the organiser's daughter. She's a bit of all right, eh?" Good heavens, I was the organiser's daughter. He was talking about me! And now my Dad has introduced us.

A little later the young man—Alex is his name—asks me to dance. He tells me that he had such a good laugh that morning when someone who works with him took leave in order to attend his mother's wedding. It really seems to tickle his fancy.

"Yes, well, my mother got married three weeks ago too," I say.

He folds in half, doubled over with laughter. I can't help laughing with him.

What I didn't know then was that we would be laughing together most days for more than fifty years to come. This is astounding, given all the trials that would come our way. At the time I had no inkling of the patience and forgiveness of which this man was capable.

Dad had got to know Alex when they stayed in a rather down-market hotel while the family was looking for a house and Alex was looking for "bachelor digs" in town. Their friendship was cemented through a shared dislike of being served sweet potatoes instead of ordinary potatoes. Neither minded sweet potatoes, but definitely not *instead* of potatoes.

Some weeks later Alex asked me to go to bioscope with him. I didn't need to invite him to meet my parents. After all, my father had introduced us.

Dad couldn't resist it. He said my name together with Alex's surname and came up with a spectacular rhyme! He laughed and said, "Makes a lovely rhyme doesn't it?"

I was really angry. "Just because he's asked me out doesn't mean I am going to marry him—even if it means I'll have a surname that rhymes with my name."

My father reminded me of that the day we got engaged. And again the day we got married.

It wasn't the rhyming surname that drew me to Alex. It was his wonderful sense of humour and sense of fun, his impeccable manners, his absolute honesty—and what girl can resist loving someone who so obviously loves her too?

Our courtship was slow and easy. Alex was working shifts at a local rubber and tyre factory and would pop into my office to see me every afternoon on his way home. I always knew when he was coming because a strong smell of rubber pervaded the air as he turned the corner to my office.

We had no money between us, no car to get around in, yet as I look back now, we had the time of our lives. We laughed every day! He visited my family and was loved by them. My young brother and sister loved him too and we spent many an evening baby-sitting them. Alex's ability to engage with really young children has always been better than mine, and he would keep them entertained right up to the time for their bedtime story. After that it was time for kissing-on-the-couch! Yet Alex was noticeably undemonstrative in public. We never held hands while walking together, and he didn't show affection in front of other people. He still doesn't. I can't recall receiving compliments from him either.

We spent days going to the beach, evenings at the movies and on Sunday evenings always made for the same little café to treat ourselves to an omelette, bacon and chips. We were engaged for a whole year, which gave us plenty of time to get to know each other and to save a little money.

Alex enjoyed a beer or two after refereeing a rugby game, and I didn't drink at all. There was no way that I was going to become like my mother. I tucked the incident with the bottle of sherry into the back of my mind, choosing to ignore the day that I had behaved exactly like my mother, and continued to frown upon drinking. I made Alex pay me a sixpence every time he drank a beer and gathered a tidy sum in my savings account, which came in handy on our honeymoon.

Yet I did learn to enjoy the odd port and lemonade, which was considered to be a genteel drink for women at the time.

CHAPTER FOURTEEN

ENGAGEMENT AND MARRIAGE

Now that we are engaged, I have come to Cape Town with Alex to meet his family. I am quite overcome by the beauty and the history of the city. At first I was very anxious, because Alex is a non-practising Jew and I didn't know how I, a gentile, would be received by his family. Yet everyone has been most warm and welcoming.

The morning that I am due to fly back home while Alex stays in Cape Town for the rest of his leave, his mother comes to my bedroom and sits down beside me as I lie in bed.

"Jean, I have something very difficult to say." I look at her, worried. Have I done something wrong, said something wrong? But no, it is far more serious than that. "I do wish you would reconsider this engagement." She speaks earnestly, and I can tell that she doesn't want to offend me but is deeply concerned. "I don't know how else to put this, but I feel that Alex's religion will prove a great stumbling block." She laughs self-consciously and adds, "You know what they say, once a Jew always a Jew." I stare at her uncomprehendingly. She goes on. "I think this has happened just because of propinquity." I don't know what "propinquity" means, but it sounds very serious. Her next words make her mission very clear. "You see, Jean, I don't think that Alex has had the opportunity to meet a Jewish girl, someone that might suit him better. All I ask is that you give him a little more time to do so before you go ahead with this marriage."

Here is another way in which I am not good enough. My heart feels as if it has turned to stone, but I take off my pretty silver solitaire diamond engagement ring and hand it to her.

"Please give this back to Alex," I say. "And please explain why I have given it to you." I can't bring myself to say any more and as she leans towards me, I turn my face to the wall.

I was really astounded at myself for taking a stand. I had always found it difficult to stand up for myself and would rather just do as I was told and go along with what other people wanted for me. I was always afraid of "rocking the boat".

Alex didn't notice that I wasn't wearing my ring as he took me to the airport later in the day and I didn't say anything to him about it. My heart was very sore for the next few days but when he returned from his holiday, he once again presented me with the ring and said that the matter was never to be spoken of again. To this day I don't know what passed between him and his mother. Yet she was always warm and loving to me and in later years said that she couldn't have chosen a better wife for her son.

I can hardly believe that I will be twenty in three days' time. Sometimes I feel a lot older and sometimes a lot younger. Today I feel a lot older.

It is my wedding day. I am alone in my room, dressed in my wedding suit of navy blue with small white polka dots. It has a neat straight skirt and the jacket has a fashionable little peplum. I have saved and managed to buy myself really smart leather shoes with high heels. And my navy gloves are the softest leather I have ever worn.

I settle my large-brimmed navy hat on my newly curled hair and don't really resent the fact that there isn't to be a wedding veil on my head. I know that I am doing the right thing in marrying Alex and that he will care for me and I for him for the rest of our days.

Mom is here for the wedding. She is sober and controlled. I imagine that she would rather have it this way, no matter how her head may ache or how strictly she needs to control her intake of alcohol, than have my father see what she has become. It is probably also important for her not to have Alex realise that she has such a devilish drinking problem.

Evelyn has been generous and helpful, turning her house over to accommodate all our arrangements. Money has been tight, and Alex and I have ordered and paid for our invitations and our wedding cake. Mom is cross about this and says that Dad should have paid, but I know that he and Evelyn really struggle financially, and we have the money saved, so it really doesn't matter. Some of it has come from the sixpences Alex paid me for every beer he consumed in the past year.

We hoped that Alex's mother would come to the wedding. That is why we didn't plan to marry in church, but at the last minute she decided that she wouldn't be coming after all.

I go to the front of the house, where everyone smiles and tells me how pretty I look and how smart my suit is. I feel the smile upon my face but I have the most awful butterflies in my stomach and I want to cry.

The car is waiting at the gate to drive us to the magistrates' court. As I step in, I feel my hat knock against the top of the door and I have to grab it quickly to stop it from falling onto the gravel of the driveway. I am so embarrassed. Alex laughs and I am cut to the quick. Why can't I just manage to be dignified and elegant on my wedding day? My face is scarlet, and I wonder if I really am good enough to be anyone's wife.

Because I am part of the legal fraternity of the town, the chief magistrate himself will marry us. We have been allowed to put flowers in the courtroom. Our friends and family follow us in a procession of cars so that they can be present at the ceremony.

Old Max, predictably, steals our thunder. He has acquired the very first Polaroid camera in town and takes pictures of the event, which are later published in the local newspaper.

Nearly fifty years later I went back to that little town, and there was the house from which we were married, simple and unassuming, with white gables and eight stone steps leading up to the front stoep. It looked fresh and cool with its white walls and pillars supporting the veranda roof. The front steps and the roof were painted green and as I looked at it, I could see my little brother and sister sitting on the bottom step on the day of my wedding. When he heard the champagne corks pop, my brother jumped up and rushed inside, calling, "What's happening, Daddy?"

I had learned to enjoy a glass of champagne by that time and must confess to enjoying the feeling of being slightly "tiddly" as I sat giggling in the car while we drove away to our honeymoon.

We had to borrow a car to go away. A kind colleague of Alex's offered us his rather elderly car and we had it polished up and serviced for the journey. The assembled company gathered around the car to see us on our way, and they managed to get a large amount of confetti over everything and into every nook and cranny of the car. One of the little triangular windows was missing so we didn't have much hope of locking it. Of course, there were tin cans tied to the back bumper and "Just married" written on the rear window. I can still hear the laughter and the cries of "Good luck!" as we were sent on our way.

Despite the polish and the service, the car managed to give trouble on the way and the day after we got to our destination, we found that we couldn't get it into any gear except reverse. We had to reverse all the way down the main street to find a garage to fix the fault.

We had saved hard for our honeymoon. We spent it at a splendid hotel in Hermanus. We felt that this was going to be a once in a lifetime opportunity to stay in such a grand hotel. It makes me smile to think that we have since been able to stay at the Palace of the Lost City and, grander still, the Mount Nelson!

There was a sad postscript to the wedding. My mother was enraged by the fact that my father had not paid for any part of the wedding and, I heard later, gave him a thorough piece of her mind after we had left for our honeymoon. He sent her a cheque for a small sum that he could barely afford, and she returned it, torn to shreds.

I know it is possible to feel the hurt of others, and to this day I can still feel my father's hurt.

CHAPTER FIFTEEN

AWAY ON OUR OWN

There are three policemen in the office. They seem belligerent and push past the reception desk straight into the office of the senior partner. I look at the others and see in their expressions what I think is a reflection of the anxiety that must be showing in my own face. What is going on?

I haven't really settled into the new company since the move to the Transvaal. Having made reasonable progress with old Max, I was able to find a place that would article me, but it isn't the same.

When Alex found a better job in the Transvaal, I transferred my articles from the Cape Law Society to the Transvaal Law Society, but things are more difficult here. The new man is no old Max. I have found myself shoved into a corner and given tedious secretarial duties. (I can type, can't I?)

But now our office is being invaded by a posse of policemen and detectives, and there is great consternation and bewilderment amongst the staff.

After about ten minutes the door opens, and the police march the boss off in handcuffs. The place is buzzing. The staff are astounded. The clients in the waiting area watch the proceedings with their mouths agape. The other partners come rushing out of their offices and then repair to the boardroom, where they stay closeted for about an hour. Calls are made through the switchboard, but even though one can listen in, no one dares to.

It appeared that the arrested senior partner had been using trust funds for his own enrichment. In the end he came to trial and was sentenced to several years in jail. The legal business closed down, and I decided that this was a sign for me to have a family and settle down to motherhood. I had started off with such great ambition and had been encouraged and assisted by old Max, but here I was now, without the energy or the courage to pick myself up and get on with reaching the goals I had set myself. I felt a failure.

The move from one town to another, a spell of staying in an hotel, looking for a flat to live in and the move into that flat, combined with days doing very boring clerical work, all militated against my trying to study and go on my articled way. These are excuses, I know, but I was young and newly married. Perhaps old Max had been right and girls were not meant for the law but rather for marriage and babies.

Alex's job in the Transvaal took us to Klerksdorp, a mining town where the miners were a tough, hard-drinking, hard-living, hard-working bunch of men. My memories of our stay in the hotel are of very bad food, corridors echoing with fights after the pubs had closed and one particular night that makes me laugh now but terrified the life out of me at the time!

Alex was the assistant town electrical engineer and when maintenance had to be done on certain installations, he would go out at midnight to oversee the work. This was so that the switch-off of electricity could be undertaken after the cinemas and pubs had closed and things were generally quiet.

As our room in the hotel had only one key, he would lock me in when he left so that he didn't have to disturb me when he returned.

On this particular evening a fight broke out in the corridor outside our room as usual, and before I was properly awake, shots were being fired! I dived under the double bed and crept into the far corner to spend the rest of the time there until Alex returned in the early hours of the morning.

Eventually we found a small flat and moved out of the hotel.

I have never been good with my hands. I can't paint, draw or sew. Maybe this isn't really true, because I can knit and embroider quite well. Nevertheless, there wasn't much fun in furnishing on a shoestring. I felt clumsy as I tried to pleat and fold the pretty cretonne with blue and yellow flowers. I chose blue and yellow thumbtacks with which to fasten the pleats to the apple boxes. We moved nine times in the first three years of our marriage, but at last we managed to buy a house and I wanted it to be as pretty as I could manage. With hands that felt as big as hams I tried to dress apple boxes to serve as bedside tables for our bedroom. My fingers were sore, and I knew that I would never be able to give those little boxes the flair and artistry that I was hoping to achieve. We had very little money. Each piece of furniture we acquired seemed like a triumph, and I wanted to treasure and appreciate it.

When I look back now, I know that the house did look pretty and my efforts with blue and yellow thumbtacks turned out very well, as did the sheeting on which I embroidered cats, dogs and rabbits in brightly coloured wool for curtains for the baby that we were expecting in October 1956. But I had not yet acquired any kind of self-confidence or a sense of self-worth, and Alex never offered any word of praise or encouragement.

Alex's sense of humour drew me to him in the first place, and his gentle way with children is another thing I love about him. He is also generous and kind. Yet I learned that Alex is completely undemonstrative and seldom, if ever, gives compliments. In much the same way he also abstains from criticising. He is a man who doesn't interfere or offer advice. The fact that this is his character had a great influence on my self-image and didn't help to take away my feeling of not being good enough.

CHAPTER SIXTEEN

BABIES

I sit embroidering bunnies on the sheeting for the baby's bedroom. I am almost cross-eyed, and my shoulders ache from the effort. I am anxious—afraid, really—of being responsible for a child.

I feel alone and desperately afraid during the delivery. The child I am bearing will be able to watch the birth of his children one day, but this was not something that happened in the 1950s. Our son is perfect, blond and cute and as beautiful as all babies are—in their mothers' eyes, at least.

The responsibilities I have worried about are enormous. Our little boy develops an abscess under his eye within the first three weeks of his life. The problem is a blocked tear duct. I sit in the discomfort of a very hot hospital ward, waiting for my baby to wake up so that I can breast-feed him. The hospital lets me know how privileged I am to be allowed to continue to feed him. "Usually," the large ward sister says, "we make you bind your breasts and put the baby on a bottle. We don't want mothers hanging around the ward, getting in our way." It isn't just sweat that drips off me in the heat. While I am waiting for him to wake up, my milk leaks and I am soaked to below my waist. I am alone, afraid and anxious, watching my little scrap of a baby fighting the heat and the pain. His cries startle me when he wakes, and I am able to pick him up and comfort him and feed him, bringing relief to us both.

I remembered that nurse's words eleven months later as I was brought into the ward of another hospital to see my child's swollen face and blackened eyes after he had had an operation to remove a soft wart from his tear duct. We were up to our eyes in medical debt by then, so we had thrown caution to the wind and insisted that I go into the hospital with the baby this time. He had had four previous operations to clear his tear duct since that first one when I was still breast-feeding him, and this time they had decided to do an exploratory operation.

At the same time they did plastic surgery to ensure that the duct stayed clear in the future. The plastic surgeon did not charge us for the operation, and we learned afterwards that he always gave his services free to cases of this nature, charging higher fees for cosmetic surgery in order to make a living.

Shortly after coming round from the anaesthetic, my baby sneezed, and I screamed as blood spattered from his nose all over him, the walls and me. Fortunately it didn't take him long to recover from the operation, but it took us years to reach any kind of financial stability again.

The car rattles and shakes over the bad road. The rain is coming down in sheets. Alex can't see where we're going, but we dare not stop for fear of getting bogged down. There's a roof rack on the car with most of our luggage on it. God alone knows how wet it's getting. I suppose we will laugh about this one day, but I can't see any funny side as I sit, sweating profusely, trying to move the windscreen wipers back and forth by hand, turning the little knob on the dashboard to and fro between my fingers. Suddenly I see the luggage carrier sliding slowly down over the windscreen. It must have been shaken loose by the bouncing of the car.

"Stop!" I call to Alex. With much cursing he gets out and wrestles with the luggage carrier while he stands ankle-deep in water.

Luckily the baby sleeps through it all, neither stirring nor crying. We are on our way to see my father to show him his first grandchild. We find him ill in bed but cheerful and pleased to see us. He turns out to be quite the doting grandpa, cooing and gurgling happily at the four-month-old little boy. He smiles and bounces the baby on his tummy, and much to everyone's delight the baby in turn gurgles and giggles.

My father had what people referred to as "Irish good looks", with dark hair and blue eyes: a handsome man, and one who loved his children with all his heart. Nothing pleased him more than to have all his kids under one roof, safe under his watchful eye. I think that he and my mother must have made a very handsome couple and in their young days they must have shared an impish sense of fun. I have never been sure what caused the rift between my mother and my father. I was always afraid to ask. I have a pretty good idea, though, that it was my mother's alcoholism.

I think that I have inherited my father's sense of family. I too am never happier than when I have my children—and now my grandchildren—close to me.

I was glad that we had made that trip to introduce Mark to his grandfather because just eighteen months later a telegram came to say that my father had died suddenly of a heart attack, and we had to make the journey again to join a devastated family at a rainy, sad and depressing funeral.

By the time my father died I had another little boy. I threw myself into being a "good housewife". I even attempted to sew, making the boys pyjamas and shirts and boxer shorts. I wasn't too good at it, but the garments were quite acceptable. I hated sewing, however. I had a stroke of luck eventually when we had a burglar come into the house in the middle of the day. All he stole was a watch and the sewing machine, but I could have thrown a party, I was so relieved.

I baked every week, filling tins with biscuits and cakes. I made ginger beer and lemon curd. I enjoyed doing that. The smell of orange cake and peanut butter cookies in the kitchen was pleasant. My friends came with their children and joined in the big bake, bringing their own ingredients and tins. A row of small people perched on the counter, waiting for their turn to lick the batter dishes. I remember the pink cheeks of the mums—my neighbours and I—brought on by the exertion of whipping and stirring and bending to retrieve trays of biscuits from the hot oven.

I even tried my hand at flower arranging. I struggled with the utter boredom of flower arranging classes, messing around with containers in different shapes, trying to make the stems of poppies or dahlias go where I wanted them to go, burning the ends first to make them last longer. Perhaps that is why today I claim that I really only admire the kind of arrangement that looks as if the blooms have been thrown carelessly into the vase.

I felt a great need to create something, to do something admirable, something that "counted", so that I might be good enough. I certainly did not achieve that through flower arranging.

We had a circle of very good friends and there was a round of parties every couple of months. We each took our own refreshments and drinks. My favourite at the time was gin and tonic. On occasion I felt that I had had a little more than I should, but I never got drunk or got into trouble through drinking. Yet somewhere in the back of my mind I knew that alcohol helped me to mix with other people, to cope with social occasions, and there were times when I would have just one secret drink before we left home for a party. I was fully aware of the dangers of what I was doing but believed that I could control myself. I was convinced that I could cope. Was I not the daughter of an alcoholic? Did I not know the dangers of alcohol and secret drinking? I would never become like my mother.

There were good times. We spent several holidays at Kenton-on-Sea, a coastal resort in the Eastern Cape. In those days it was unspoilt and uncrowded. There was no electricity in the town and our water supply came from rainwater collected in tanks.

We had lazy days on the beach, long afternoon walks amongst the rocks at the river mouth and generally loved being a family having fun together. We played games by lamplight at night and loved each other with all our hearts.

CHAPTER SEVENTEEN

BREAKING AWAY

I knew then, as I still know today, that being there for the children was something that "counted", yet I chafed at having only the SABC Women's Hour or my library books to occupy my mind. I decided that I would attempt to study for a BA degree in psychology and English by correspondence.

During that time my mind expanded like those folded bits of paper that you put in children's bath water and watch as they grow plump and pretty, changing into flowers or butterflies. I experienced great joy in reading and thinking, finding meaning in things that I had never considered before.

It wasn't easy. I dropped the children at nursery school and went to study in the local library. The quietness, the studious air of the place, touched me, and I savoured the time I spent there. I felt that I needed an alarm clock to alert me when it was time to fetch the children and go back to my other life.

But, unlike the attorneys' exams that old Max had helped me through, there was no one to share the experience with, no one who seemed to care whether I achieved anything at all, or who even recognised that I was capable of achieving anything. Maybe this was all my own doing. I stayed inside my cocoon, too afraid to share what I was experiencing for fear of being ridiculed for reaching for things that I didn't deserve, for not being good enough. Alex never gave me any indication that he felt that what I was doing was important, or even difficult—which it was!

Once I had successfully completed my exams, I went back to flower arranging. I developed strange perceptual problems. When I picked up a glass or a cup, I would knock it over more often than I was able to grasp it safely. My doctor sent me to a neurologist, who sent me to a psychiatrist, who, after three visits, told me to do myself—and him—a favour and get myself a job. He believed that I just needed mental stimulation. I began looking for a job that I could do part-time and that would allow me to stay at home and not work if the children were sick or needed me. With my knowledge of psychology I was able to get work moderating focus groups, and my involvement in marketing research grew from that. Once I got into the swing of having an interest outside of the home, all my perceptual problems disappeared. It seemed that the psychiatrist's diagnosis had been correct.

Eventually I got a mornings-only job in an advertising agency. The people were fun and lively, and working in the agency made me feel as if I was with the avant-garde crowd. The field I was in brought me into contact with dozens of different people with different views. I could feel my perspectives change, and I began to believe that I had a place in the world.

CHAPTER EIGHTEEN

THE START OF THE SLIPPERY SLOPE

It is a quiet, sunny highveld Sunday: Valentine's Day. The sky is blue and cloudless. I am standing on the lawn, waving goodbye to friends who came by for a drink. I can hear the splashing and the laughter of the kids in the pool. I feel content, I feel pretty and even good enough to be part of this family. It doesn't matter that I seldom receive compliments. It doesn't even matter that I have never in my life received a Valentine's card from anyone. It dawns on me that the drinks I had this afternoon are helping me to feel "good enough". I have a real physical sense of the alcohol lifting me up and removing me from my own anxieties. I feel as if I am floating above the ground and, after a lifetime of feeling responsible for whatever went wrong in my world, I suddenly feel "good enough".

It didn't strike me then but I know today that the drinks I sneaked before parties and the fact that I liked to pour drinks for friends so that I could pour a little extra into my own glass were not only because I felt that alcohol gave me confidence to mix with others, but what I was doing was also typical alcoholic behaviour.

Anyone looking at me that day would have sworn that I had everything I could wish for and should have been more than happy and content with my lot. He or she would probably have been right. Yet the feeling of having been robbed of something played on my mind. I don't know whether I felt unloved, whether I was aware that I had lacked nurturing as a child or whether my lack of confidence and self-worth was what plagued me day in and day out. What the cause of my discontent was doesn't really matter now. That is how I felt and I didn't know how to deal with it.

I went straight inside and poured myself another—secret—drink. Gone were the memories of the secret drinks I had poured myself at the age of sixteen. I had forgotten about the consequences of that occasion. I was desperate to maintain the sense of freedom and self-worth that lifted me up when I drank.

It was part of the culture of the advertising agency to go to the pub for lunch. It was there that I discovered the same sort of feeling that that glass of sherry had given me on my sixteenth birthday. The bar lunches used to start at one and end at two. For a while—then they would start at twelve and end at two thirty. Gradually my stay at the bar stretched further into the afternoons, and within a year or so I would be there for the whole afternoon.

I was always full of stories about how much work I had and how it required of me to spend longer hours at the office. I didn't get home totally drunk every day. I managed to keep an alcoholic "buzz" going without losing control.

I had a well-trained maid at home, who cooked the dinner and looked after the children in the afternoons, and this helped me to keep up the image of being able to cope.

My colleagues and the people I met in the pubs seemed to like me. They thought I was clever, bought me drinks and listened to what I had to say. The sound of laughter and the clinking of glasses, the backslapping, the jokes, were all a kind of camaraderie that I had never known. I had been a shy young girl at nineteen, married at twenty and a mother of two at twenty-five. An unplanned baby at twenty-nine was difficult to cope with, no matter how dearly I loved him when he dramatically burst upon the scene by Caesarean section.

I know now that I could never have spent time in those drinking places—"watering holes", we cleverly called them—without alcohol. I was too shy, too inhibited, too trapped behind my "curtain". But the alcohol worked for me, and I needed more and more to bolster my self-confidence. Alcohol helped me feel in tune with the world.

Alex didn't complain, although I realise now that he worried about and disapproved of my behaviour. Maybe he realised that my job was helping me stay out of the rut of looking after children, baking and arranging flowers day after day.

And so I was drawn into the squirrel cage of alcoholism. It happened gradually, yet it seemed that the more I drank the more I needed to drink; the more I needed to keep me on the plane where I felt I was "good enough", where I could talk to people, laugh with people.

Many people believe that excessive stress will lead one to drink excessively. This may be true, and many people might become heavy drinkers for that reason. But alcoholism is a disease—recognised as such by the World Health Organisation. I know many people who speak of alcohol helping them to cope with shyness and lack of confidence and giving them courage to mix with the world around them. That's how it was for me.

It is absolutely true that alcohol will erase your memory of what you said and did the night before. Events are completely blanked out. Often others don't even notice this and can't believe it when the alcoholic has no recollection of what he or she did the night before. It is a fact that an alcoholic will feel and display utter remorse and really mean it at the time, promising "never to do it again" but it is also a fact that, while still drinking, he or she is quite incapable of keeping that promise.

Life gradually became a series of fragmented nightmares: frequent episodes caused by alcohol and kept at bay by drinking more.

I had lost control.

CHAPTER NINETEEN

LOSING THE WAY

I am standing at the dining room window, looking out at the fruit trees in the back garden. The weather is warm and sunny and the trees are in blossom. Soon there will be apricots and peaches and plums to pick, the jam will be boiling on the stove, filling the kitchen with sweet, fruity smells. I am shaking both inside and on the outside. I know that I am going to die. I know that I will never cope with the picking of the fruit or the making of the jam.

I am terrified and I don't know which way to turn. My days are completely obsessed with obtaining—and hiding—bottles of liquor. I sometimes hide them so successfully that I hide them even from myself. Some nights I know that I still have some left but cannot for the life of me remember where I have hidden the bottles.

I decide to put the bottles in the linen cupboard, which has only one key. I lock the cupboard and keep the key in my pocket. This is my other obsession—I won't wear anything that doesn't have a pocket. And so badly do I need that liquor that

I keep the key in my hand, inside my pocket. I can't "trust" the key to stay where it is until the next time I need it. I have to have control over it, because the worst thing that can happen to me is that I will be left without alcohol for more than an hour at a time.

Day after day I obsess, making sure that I won't run out of alcohol. I know every bottle store in our neighbourhood and on the way to and from my place of work. I don't want the staff in the bottle stores to realise that I have a drinking problem, so I change the places of purchase, rotating them, making sure that I don't go into the same one day after day.

I walk into one of my "chosen" bottle stores, and the assistant turns around and takes a bottle of my brand of vodka off the shelf and puts it down in front of me. I am enraged! What right does this woman have to assume that I want vodka on this particular day? I snatch the bottle from her, thrust the money over the counter and leave the bottle store in a hurry, not bothering to wait for my change. How many bottles have I bought from this store? I cannot remember, but that still gives her no right to presume that she knows what I am here for.

I am outside a cinema. The crowd is waiting for the doors to open. There's an expectant murmuring, an air of excitement. Mingled perfumes scent the air and the men's dinner suits complement the elegance of the women's evening dresses. Have I blanked out again? I have no recollection of how I got here. As I "come to", I am not sure what I am supposed to be doing. I look down and see that I am in evening dress: a long black, rather elegant dress in African style, with beadwork down the front. The hem has come undone halfway around the bottom. Under the trailing hem I see my shoes, one black and one brown.

What many people don't know is that drunks can operate in what is called a "blankout" and still seem to be functioning "normally". I doubt if anyone noticed the black and the brown shoe. I was wearing a long dress with the hem undone, which was possibly hiding my shoes. Speak to any woman and you will hear her tell of how she has on occasion caught her shoe in the hem of her skirt while getting out of a car. That is what might have happened in this case. Besides, when people are standing in a crowd, not many can see below the waists of those around them.

I learn later that we had tickets to the premiere of a movie in aid of a charity. I can't remember how I got there, how I managed to dress, why the hem was hanging loose. I don't remember what the movie was about or how I got home again. I know that Alex was with me and obviously he drove us home, but I must have blanked out, because I don't remember much else.

I do know that Alex didn't berate me, accuse me or say anything to me about the incident. I hadn't actually misbehaved. A loose hem and odd shoes could hardly be classed as misbehaviour. I have inadvertently worn odd shoes when stone cold sober, after all—and it has made people laugh, not feel ashamed.

I try to play the piano, but my hands shake so badly that I can't play a note. I know that if I have a drink, the shakes will go away. I go to the linen cupboard and swig vodka straight from the bottle. Gradually the shakes subside and I sit at the piano again and start to play. How good it is to be able to do this. It's not long before I have to have another swig from that bottle and then another and another.

Eventually, after some years, the time came when I was not able to play the piano much at all because I could not coordinate my fingers with the notes. I had to give in to the shakes and give up trying to play. I was intensely aware of my inability to play the piano—music had buoyed me up in many situations, but I was unable to connect to it any longer.

I didn't know whether my own children loved me. I believed that I still functioned for them and that people didn't know of my shame and guilt, but the blankouts were happening all the time. I would wake up each morning and not remember what had happened the night before. I made dinner dates and forgot to keep them.

It is quite late at night. I am in the kitchen, drinking directly from a bottle of wine. The door opens and in comes my eldest son. We both freeze.

"Oh!" he says.

"Oh!" I reply.

He goes to the fridge and helps himself to a glass of water, turns his back on me and leaves, closing the door behind him. I swig from the bottle again as if nothing has happened.

At meetings I make notes furiously because I know I can no longer trust myself to remember the gist of what has been decided. The next day I am quite incapable of reading my own handwriting.

I have been drinking during my lunch hour and return to my office, rather boisterous and loud. One of my colleagues asks me, in a joking fashion, whether I have been drinking. I answer the question with loud laughter and say, "Of course, I drink through my lunch hour every day." She just laughs and treats it as a joke. After that, I am careful not to get too loud when she is around.

My fingers tremble so badly that I cannot fasten the buttons on my blouse in the mornings. I need an early morning drink to steady them.

I don't go anywhere without making sure that I have alcohol available. I keep my bottles in big handbags that go everywhere with me. I sometimes put gin into a Tupperware container so that I can seal it with the lid and carry it in my handbag without fear that it might spill. I make many trips to the cloakrooms, where I can have a swig of my chosen drink of the day straight from the bottle.

The problem of getting rid of the bottles becomes insurmountable. I race down the motorway to Pretoria to fetch my sons from boarding school, having stayed sober for the journey, a suitcase full of empty vodka bottles in the boot. I stop amongst the blue-gum trees at the side of the road and hurl bottles into the waste can meant for picnickers. I try to be furtive about it, hoping that no one will notice. I feel guilty and ashamed and I don't want anyone to guess what I am doing. The following week the suitcase is full of bottles again.

Years later Alex told me how he had once found six empty beer cans in the back of the car. He had been horrified and had positively trembled at the thought that, had the police had occasion to stop me, or had I had an accident and they had been found, I would have been in serious trouble. I still find it strange that he said nothing to me at the time.

Nevertheless, I know that confrontation is one of the hardest things for the family of an alcoholic. In a book by Ruth

Maxwell called *The Booze Battle* (first published by Praeger Publishers Inc. in 1976), one reads about this phenomenon:

> Our society finds many reasons why a man may drink more than he should. There's his high-pressure job, tense working conditions, monotonous routine, combined business-martini lunches, commuting, demanding wife, unpaid bills. What reasons can a woman have?

It's difficult to find any. Usually husbands and children think her drinking is due to some family problem that will be solved in time. Meantime, however, she should cut down on her drinking or stop completely, and she is to blame if she doesn't.

> Husbands and children overlook alcoholism as the problem. They do not want to believe that their wives and mothers are alcoholics. The idea is very difficult for them to acknowledge and accept even if they were to suspect it, and they will help her hide the drinking to escape discovery and disgrace. They will exert great efforts to keep her and her problem hidden as long as they can.

> The alcoholic wife and mother also suffers acute feelings of shame concerning her drinking. She knows well how society views her. Like her family members she will blame herself until eventually self-blame and self-recrimination cause a deeper surrender to her addiction. She will keep her

drinking a secret for as long as she is able. She will
drink quietly and alone; and she will hide it until it
can no longer be hidden.

Finding this book was interesting to me. The year 1976 was right in the middle of my alcoholic period. The author relates a case study about a man (Ken) who believed that his wife had been secretly drinking for several years. I recognised my own behaviour. I would race to take our guests' glasses and offer to get them a refill while I got one for myself. In this way I could be sure to pour myself a really stiff drink—sometimes without any mixer at all. I would sneak drinks from the drinks cabinet and water down what was left in the bottle—or manage to replace a full bottle before its disappearance was noticed. When Ken—the man in the book—questioned his wife, she would

blame it on the maids or women who had come
to lunch. Ken, like most husbands, accepted her
explanations even though he did not always
believe her. He wanted to believe her. It was too
difficult for him to do otherwise. Her drinking was
as unacceptable to her as it was to those around
her. She was powerless to stop herself and too
ashamed to ask for help.

I can identify so strongly with the words "she was powerless to stop herself". That is exactly the case with all alcoholics. We are powerless to stop ourselves and very definitely too ashamed to ask for help.

Another quote from *The Booze Battle* resonates with me:

There is evidence that many husbands . . . put up
with a lot while avoiding treatment for themselves
or their mates . . . [T]he wife is not forced into
treatment for her disease, for she is not considered
sick or worthy of help.

I know that today, thirty years after that book was written, there is greater understanding of the disease of alcoholism, yet I doubt whether people are able to confront the issue any more courageously than at that time.

I believe now that Alex doesn't like confronting issues. He appeared to be turning a blind eye to things that upset him, but I think that his hurt or irritation, or whatever it was, showed itself in rage against less important issues. His temper flared easily and the whole family feared his rages, which were very often about issues that didn't warrant such anger.

I suspect that had he raged at me, confronted me, threatened to leave me or—best of all—told me that he loved me and that my drinking was hurting us all, I would have made the effort sooner to do something about it.

I was ashamed of what I was doing, yet I had no control over it and when it was seemingly ignored, I thought that I could get away with it—or that no one but I cared about it.

Recently I was reminiscing about some company cars that I had driven and talked about "my Alfa Romeo". Alex immediately contradicted me and said that I had never driven an Alfa. In fact, I had two Alfas during my drinking days and the denial made me wonder whether he had been able just to ignore most of what I was doing while he concentrated on carrying on with his own life. I know that I was terribly aware of the fact that he never looked at me. I would watch him as his eyes skirted my face even while he was talking directly to me. I presumed that I was so ugly in my addiction that he couldn't bear the sight of me.

Yet that was not the only thing that kept him from confronting me. It is a very difficult thing to confront anyone who is drinking too much. Alcoholism is not known as a "disease of denial" for nothing. Not only does the alcoholic deny it, but family and friends seem to turn a blind eye too. It is almost as if they cannot believe or come to terms with the fact that this is happening to them. The feeling seems to be that the drinking might be a result of stress, unhappiness, depression or anything that doesn't count as a "moral problem".

It wasn't only Alex who skirted the issue. I used to love telephoning all sorts of people when I was drunk and having long conversations with them. I used to phone one of my close cousins in England. Years later, when I confessed to her that I was an alcoholic, she told me that she had known for a long time and that when I had phoned her, it had been quite obvious that I was drunk. She also told me that one of my sons, when visiting her in England, had told her that I was drinking "a lot" and that he thought it was because of family pressures.

My mother's sisters never referred to the fact that she drank heavily. Neither did I, of course. Even Joe, although vilified and criticised for the way he treated my mother, was never called an alcoholic. Mothers who drink are hidden away from the world, and no one in the family ever mentioned my mother's alcoholism. Alex and I both knew that she drank uncontrollably—as did Joe—yet we never discussed it with each other or anyone else. I never talked about it to my mother's sisters either, and they didn't mention it to me. In fact, we only began to talk about it after she had died as a result of her heavy drinking.

It occurs to me that my grandfather, to my knowledge, never confronted my mother about her drinking—or Joe's—either.

A friend told me that she had once heard someone say that the family of alcoholics behave as though there is a huge bottle sitting right in the middle of the living room, with everyone just walking around it as if it doesn't exist.

There are those who are called "high bottom drunks" and those who are known as "low bottom drunks". The former are people like me. I had money in the bank, a job, a car in the garage. I earned enough money at the time to be able to pay for each of my children to participate in a school tour to Europe that was organised by their school. And, of course, I had money for liquor. Only close family members knew that I drank too much, and they just kept avoiding the bottle in the middle of the living room.

Somehow I managed not to kill myself or my children in my motorcar. I grew obese because, unlike some drunks, I didn't stop eating while I was drinking.

I could tell no one about my fear and guilt and shame. I knew that many people would view me as immoral, weak-willed and lying, deserving of neither sympathy nor help. How could they not, when this was the only way in which I saw myself? The maze I was in had no exit and I resigned myself to lying down to die, right there in the middle of the puzzle. I could see no way out.

My mouth is dry. I am dying of thirst. This is easy to believe, because I feel like death anyway. Eventually I identify the droning in my head—the sound of aeroplane engines. I can't place where I am. I force my eyelids open and find that I am, indeed, on an aeroplane. But where I am going and where I have come from I have no idea. I wonder how I made it onto the plane. Do I have luggage? Frantically I feel around for my handbag and find it at my feet, intact, nothing missing.

I struggle to place myself in time, but my memory has gone missing altogether. A stewardess's face appears above me and she asks if I need anything. I croak a request for a glass of water and she smiles knowingly. I hate her. She knows that I boarded the plane drunk. I wonder if I have been snoring and maybe even drooling while I have been asleep.

I can't bring myself to ask her where the plane is headed. I will just have to hope that when we disembark I will be able to recognise the airport. I don't allow myself to think about what I will do if I can't. What will I do if I stand at the baggage carousel and can't find a bag that belongs to me?

I am asked to leave only one job and my drinking is not mentioned as the reason for my dismissal. I am enraged about it at the time. My boss calls me in and tells me that my services are no longer needed. I know that my dismissal must be because of my drinking on the job, and yet he doesn't accuse me of doing so. I just pack up my things and move on.

Years later I find myself on an aeroplane, seated next to the man who fired me. I set out to tell him how sorry I am for my behaviour and to make amends to him. He surprises me by saying that he had no idea that I was drinking too much. He just knew that I wasn't doing my job efficiently.

I manage to find another job very soon and leave that one fairly speedily when my boss says to me one day: "Jean, you have a problem." Before she comes right out and says what she thinks my problem is, I resign and move on to another position.

This one is tailor-made for me. The man to whom I am responsible drinks more than I do—and I know it.

CHAPTER TWENTY

THE FAMILY

Through all this time Alex was amazingly patient. I know that he was desperately worried about the situation and that he suffered terribly as a result of my alcoholic behaviour. Small things worried him, he has told me since. He noticed that I would take a handful of peanuts from a bowl and shake them in my hand to get rid of the salt. He realised that I must have learned this from male drinking buddies in the pubs. I do this with peanuts to this day and was never aware of its being a particularly "masculine" habit.

Alex spent many an evening phoning the hospitals and police stations, thinking that I must have been in an accident. Often I didn't come home until the early hours of the morning. If the boys were home for the holidays, Alex would see to their supper and bedtimes.

My excuses for coming home late were always related to my work. It is true that the kind of work I was involved in required being at the office at least until about nine thirty or ten at night about three nights a week.

I will never understand how Alex managed to keep going, yet he seemed to have had fierce control of himself, never confronting me and seldom pouring the contents of my bottles down the sink. Sometimes he found bottles hidden in the big cooking pots below the kitchen sink and he would put the bottles out in full view so that I would see that he had found them. Yet he never spoke to me about them. When I found them there, I would cringe inwardly, but I just got rid of them immediately and continued as if nothing had happened. To this day I do not know why he didn't talk to me about the matter.

In a way this was good—when I found them there, I was really scared that he might leave me. Alex has told me that he did consider leaving me, but somehow he hung on in the hope that I would come to my senses.

I have learned that the best way to deal with an alcoholic in your life is not to nag, accuse or threaten. Wives should not phone bosses to tell them that their hung-over husband is sick. Spouses—no matter how difficult this seems—should let their partners deal with their own problems. When alcoholics get into trouble through their drinking, they will eventually realise that it *is* the drinking that is making their lives difficult, and not fate or bad luck.

Once alcoholics realise that it is their drinking that is getting them into trouble, they are more likely to want to stop. Alex seemed to have a built-in realisation of this. Perhaps he knew it instinctively.

On one occasion I fell asleep at the wheel and drove my car into a ditch. Luckily no one was hurt. Alex came to fetch me and, as he drove me home, he told me that he knew I had been drinking, which I, of course, vehemently denied. He didn't push the point.

Another time I lost control of the car and ended up in the middle of a traffic island with a damaged back wheel. It was late at night and I had to walk to the local railway station to phone Alex to come to fetch me. I told him that I had had to swerve to avoid a dog.

I still feel shame and regret about the time that I was driving my two elder sons, who were home on vacation from university. I had been working late and had been drinking. My driving was erratic, and my elder son called out, "Mom! What are you doing?" I stopped the car and asked him to drive. The poor young man was full of apologies, but I had a great sense of relief. I still feel sad that he had felt the need to apologise for what had been a very sensible reaction.

I was mostly a "quiet" drunk, I think. I didn't make scenes or get into noisy arguments. I know now that several of my friends worried about me, yet at the time no one ever challenged me or accused me of drinking too much.

Alcoholism is a "disease of denial". Not only do the sufferers deny that they have it, but family and friends deny it too. None of us left school saying that we wanted to be alcoholics while our friends were aspiring to be lawyers, doctors, teachers or engineers. People don't want to admit that their husband or wife is an alcoholic. The sufferer gets hidden away from the world.

In our case it was a disease that was not just denied, but actually seemed to be ignored. I cannot imagine what Alex went through during that time, yet he behaved as if he believed that the problem would go away if he ignored it. I can only suppose that, while life managed to struggle on without actual harm to any of us, he managed to get through his days.

I think that in Alex's case he didn't know what to do, where to turn. Or he might just have found it terribly difficult to criticise or confront me. That has always been his way.

As for my children, it was only much later that I started to wonder how they had been affected. I have talked with them since and have been both amazed and relieved to hear that, although they couldn't deny that I had drunk too much, they never in their own minds labelled me "alcoholic". It seems that I was able to keep control at times when I really needed to.

For example, Alex had to be away overnight quite frequently on business. I always managed to control my drinking so that I was able to spend time with whichever of the children were home from boarding school, see to their meals and then drink only late at night after they—and I—had retired for the night.

One of my children needed orthodontic work and I used to fetch him from boarding school once a week to take him to the dentist in Johannesburg. I was careful not to have more than one or two small drinks during the morning and would be sober when I drove him to his appointment. It was on the way back that I began to crave alcohol, and I would speed a bit to get him back to school so that I could take my bottle out of the boot and have a strong drink before I drove myself home alone.

CHAPTER TWENTY-ONE

"MOMMY, MOMMY, MOMMY!"

The struggle to keep going was at its most difficult when my mother died. Joe phoned to say that she was very ill indeed. He asked me to go to their home to see what could be done for her. I found her emaciated and completely unable to do anything for herself. She had soiled the bed in which she was lying, and Joe was shouting at her, berating her for her lack of control. There was no mistaking that she was dying. And there was no mistaking that she was dying from the disease of alcoholism. I suppose that, if you did not know about her drinking habits, you might have put her yellow colour down to a liver disease—which was, of course, what she had. I called the doctor and when he saw her, he asked me to make arrangements to get her to hospital.

When the doctor came, he took Joe aside and asked him if she had been drinking excessively. Joe told me this later and proudly said that he had denied it.

My mother's final illness lasted about three months. She was in hospital for four weeks.

Every second day I drive from the town where we live to visit my mother in hospital. She tells me that she has seen "a sweet little mouse" running along the picture rails in her private ward. The room is full of flowers and Joe has bought her pretty nighties and bed jackets to wear. There is no end to his kindness between his bouts of horrible abuse. Many people believe that butter wouldn't melt in his mouth.

I travel that road to the hospital with a bottle of vodka on the seat beside me, swigging at it every now and then. I have sufficient control not to get fall-down drunk—after all, I am driving. Yet I manage to keep an "edge" to the way I feel. I tell myself that I need the "shot" to keep me steady and able to handle what is happening to my mother.

As I drive, I can see my mother's yellow face, her sunken cheeks and glazed eyes. I know for sure that I am headed that way if I do not stop drinking. But I am not able to. I can't believe that I can't help myself. Once I have that first drink, I have to go on drinking. I am on a path to which there seems to be no end, from which there is no escape.

The day comes when they call from the hospital to say that my mother has fallen into a coma. I rush to her side. I am distressed and anxious. When I reach the hospital, the doctor tells me that she probably has only about twenty-four hours of life left.

Joe is inconsolable. He cries and wails as if they have had the perfect life together. I hate him more than ever at this moment. I can recall bloody scenes in which he caused the blood. I feel again the chill of emergency rooms where I sat with my mother while they set a fractured arm, bound cracked ribs and tended to innumerable black eyes. After I was married, she would sometimes call me to help her get to a doctor, and I would sit in the emergency room with her. The surroundings were always sterile, frightening and cold.

I can remember the fear and suffering and guilt in her eyes as she spat at Joe: "You bastard!" I remember the night when he punched me and then pushed me down a flight of stairs, knocking out one of my front teeth.

She doesn't die. After three days she comes out of the coma, and Joe takes her off to the seaside where she can sit in a wheelchair and watch the waves and the children on the beach.

I get the call at work. It is ten o'clock in the morning. Joe's voice sounds very matter of fact in my ear: "If you want to see your mother alive, you'd better get to the hospital fast." He didn't let me know that they had returned from the coast. I didn't know that she was back in hospital.

The tyres whine on the tarmac as I break the speed limit on my way to Pretoria. There is a sour taste in my mouth and my heart thumps in my chest. I have a hangover, and the guilt and shame that fill my mind and heart are almost too much to bear. I think of crashing the car into the pillars of a bridge and joining my mother in death. If this disease has taken her, it will surely take me too, because once I have one drink, I can't stop. I simply have to have more.

It never occurs to me not to start—that that might be the key to recovery. Nobody has told me that alcoholism is a disease and not a moral problem. Yet somewhere in the back of my mind there lurks the idea that I can learn from this, stop drinking and turn my life around.

I need not die in a hospital, seeing mice running around on the picture rails. I just need to get to my mother, to put my arms around her, tell her that I love her and that I forgive her for wasting her life and her vitality, her intelligence and beauty.

"You're too late." Joe's voice comes to me through the open window of the car.

The heat is oppressive, and I see the wavy lines of a pool of water on the paving of the car park. It is a mirage, and suddenly it seems as if that is all that my life has ever been: a mirage.

Joe wails and tears at his clothes and I look at him in disgust. I know that, just as all those years ago he was able to say, "Jean has been pushed off and everything is rosy", so he feels satisfied today that I will not have the opportunity to take leave of the mother that I love so much.

I drive home in a daze, knowing for sure that I am destined for a similar ignominious and painful death if I'm not able to stop drinking. Alone in the car, I open my mouth wide and scream: "Mommy, Mommy, Mommy!" into the ether. I am hopeless and bereft. I don't know which way to turn. I have neither a mother nor a father. I feel as if I have never had either. Now there is only Joe and Evelyn, who is many miles away.

I don't have a drink for the rest of that day. I feel absolute elation as I realise that I have managed it! I can't be an alcoholic. Alcoholics drink every day, don't they?

The next day I get drunk again.

My hand trembles as I run my finger down the page. The letters are fuzzy and I struggle to read the names. The letters in the telephone directory seem blurred. My ears are ringing and my heart is beating so fast that I fear it's going to jump right out of my chest. With sweaty palms, I manage to find the name I'm looking for. I know this person to be a member of Alcoholics Anonymous and I know that if I phone her, she will help me. But I am so ashamed and embarrassed that I simply cannot get my fingers to dial. I sit at the phone for a long time. My hair is greasy in my neck—from sweat. I know that my sweat smells of vodka. I know that I am an alcoholic wreck, fat and smelly, greasy-haired, shivering and ready to die.

Many people find it very difficult to contact Alcoholics Anonymous. There is a stigma attached to alcoholism and this stigma seems to be passed on to one's membership of AA. Many people ridicule AA meetings and what takes place there. Others seem to think that they know about these things without actually having experienced them. It is one of the hardest things in the world to pick up the phone, dial the number for Alcoholics Anonymous and ask for help.

CHAPTER TWENTY-TWO

THE BEGINNING
OF THE END

It seems strange that I didn't care how many people saw me
drunk, but I was too ashamed to make a call for help and to be
seen going to a meeting of Alcoholics Anonymous. I ended up
not making the call to that person I knew who was a member.

I shook uncontrollably. I tried to control my shaking, but
alcoholic trembling is not something over which you have any
control. I was terribly afraid. I was afraid of talking to Alex
and asking him to help me do something about my drinking. I
was afraid not to talk to him. I was afraid to live. I was afraid
to die. I was afraid of what would happen to me if I stopped
drinking and even more afraid of what would happen to me if
I did not stop drinking.

I sat on the end of the bed, fat and shaking and afraid. To
my surprise, I could hear the birds singing in the garden. The
sun shone through the window and warmed my back.

I come to, fighting for air, gasping and gurgling, feeling as if I'm drowning. Something is over my head and my face, and I can't breathe. My head aches and I can taste vomit in the back of my throat. I know that if I don't remove whatever it is across my face and head, I will suffocate and die.

I give one almighty heave and move away from under the weight bearing down on me. I am lying on my back in my bed. I passed out drunk last night and now I find my husband leaning over me with a pillow in his hands. He looks terrified and white in the moonlight. I sit up, pulling air into my lungs in great heaving, shuddering breaths.

He has been trying to suffocate me. An absolute rage seizes me, but I have enough control over myself not to strike back at him. All I am able to do is sink back into the bedclothes and curl up in anguish at what I have become and what I have brought him to.

I can't really blame him. Our happy marriage, our friendship, the joy we shared in our three young sons have all been destroyed by my drinking. Oh God! I am just like my mother.

I suspect that all the control he has applied to himself, all the things that he didn't say or do about my drinking have come to the surface in one final act of rage and desperation.

I must have been snoring loudly (I often did when I fell asleep drunk) and Alex must have reached a state where he did not know what on earth to do about the awful situation that dragged on day after day. I am sure that his intention was not to kill me, but rather to do something so drastic that it would bring me to my senses.

He succeeded that night. When I had fought my way out of the dark and the lack of air, I was stone cold sober.

In retrospect even the most bizarre and devastating episodes can seem quite comical. Alex and I have laughed about that terrible night. He talked about the situation and said how glad he was that he had come to his senses and stopped, remarking, "Otherwise where would I be today?"

To which I retorted: "And what about *me*?" Then we both laughed! There has been laughter, but it came after a long hard haul back to normality.

It was Alex's act of desperation that really brought me to the point of understanding and admitting to my alcoholism. My husband is a loving, kind man and has never been violent in any way—in fact, he abhors violence. If he had been driven to such hopelessness by my behaviour, then, surely, it was time that I did something about it? I really don't know how he managed to keep going during the years that I was drinking so heavily. It must have been a huge burden for him, and the anxiety about our children must surely have weighed heavily on his shoulders.

His desperate struggle to keep our family life going without confrontation and accusation culminated in his being frustrated beyond measure.

The next morning I lie in bed for a very long time, thinking. There must be more to life than the contents of a bottle. I have lived in a bottle for the past five years—just me, inside that bottle. There has been no room for anyone or anything else. The bottle has become my whole life and I have no idea how to escape.

In a flash of insight it comes to me. I have to admit to how I feel, to what I am doing. I walk through to the lounge, where Alex is reading the paper. "Alex" I say, "I need help."

"Yes," he replies, "with your drinking."

It is the first time that my problem has been openly referred to between us.

CHAPTER TWENTY-THREE

SEEKING HELP

Sam, our doctor, gets up and closes the door to his consulting room. I have just told him that I think I am an alcoholic. I am not sure why he closed the door. Maybe it's to protect me from the ears of the folk who are sitting in the waiting room. But when he says, "Don't worry, we'll write it on your card as 'nervous anxiety'," I realise that perhaps he is making sure that he will get paid for the visit.

It's the 1970s and medical aids don't pay for the treatment of alcoholism. Nevertheless, he gives me the best piece of advice I have ever been—or will ever be—given. "I want you to go to Alcoholics Anonymous," he says. My heart sinks. What will I do amongst those deadbeats? How can someone who went to a "good" school mix with people who have come in off the streets and out of the parks?

"They're drunk!" I hear those words in my head again, see that door closing in my face. The picture of that night when I was fifteen has embedded itself in my memory. I believe that, where drunkenness is present, doors will always be slammed.

Such was my own desperation, that I followed Sam's instructions immediately. I found the number in the telephone directory and phoned Alcoholics Anonymous. A gentle, sympathetic voice at the other end of the phone told me that someone would pick me up and take me to a meeting that night. I had to steady myself by taking a drink before I went to that meeting—but I stuck to only one.

The door to the hall was open—not closed to me, as I had feared. As I entered, I found it almost full of chattering, smiling people. "Where are the alcoholics?" I wondered. Here were smiling, well-dressed people, who looked happy and serene.

I don't remember much about that meeting, except that everyone welcomed me and told me that if I thought I had a drinking problem, then I was in the right place. No one called me an alcoholic or even seemed interested in how much I drank. They told me that if I wanted what they had, then I should listen to what they had done to recover from the disease of alcoholism and try to do the same things myself.

I often laugh today because I remember that there was a beautiful woman at that meeting. I learned later that she had been a dancer when she was younger. She was wearing the most elegant pair of red high-heeled strappy sandals. Wanting what she had stopped for me, on that first night, at her pretty sandals!

Someone offered to fetch me the next night to go to another meeting, but I felt that once that week was enough and told them that I would call them when I was ready to go to a meeting again.

When I got home, I told Alex what had happened and what they had done and said and what they had read from their Big Book. I found it fascinating stuff and was convinced that, having been to that meeting, I would from now on be able to control my drinking.

One week later I was standing at the kitchen window again, sweating but cold, shivering and afraid that I was going to die in the next half-hour.

It seemed I needed to go to another meeting in order to get the hang of how to get my drinking under control. I sat through several meetings, listening to what they read and what they said. The stuff they talked about was always good for a laugh, but I knew that I would never be able to come clean about the things that I had done and felt and thought during my drinking bouts. It was all right for them, they were alcoholics, but I just turned up at these meetings to learn how to drink like a lady.

And so I continued to drink. For about three months I tried to control my drinking, but the nature of my disease was such that I couldn't do it for long and, although I always drank a little less on the days that I went to meetings, I would still arrive at the meetings drunk.

I arrive for the meeting well under the weather. It happens to be a "business" meeting, at which half an hour or so is spent just looking at how the group is run, how it is paying its bills (AA is self-supporting and does not accept outside funds), who is going to look after the library, and so on. A long and boring agenda that has nothing to do with me or my problems. What's the point of being here?

I am really angry. Here I am, looking for help to stop drinking and there they are, talking about money.

I stand up. "You're doing absolutely nothing to help me. This meeting, all these meetings, they're just a complete waste of time. I'm leaving."

Instead of leaping up and begging me to stay, they all look at me in a rather bored fashion, and one of them says, "Okay, cheers. You know where to find us if you need us."

I rush out into the parking lot and begin to look for my car. It has vanished. Up and down the rows I go, and it is nowhere to be found. Completely exasperated (nothing is going right for me tonight), I go back to the meeting. I interrupt. "You'll have to help me find my car," I tell them. My voice is strident.

A couple of faces look my way. "Sh!" says one. "Sit down, keep quiet and listen. We'll help you after the meeting."

It's a small thing, but it makes me stop and think. These people are here to get sober and save their own and each other's lives. After the meeting they help me find my car. (It is in the upstairs car park and I have been searching the one downstairs.)

I drive home, mortified and angry. I thought they wouldn't know I was drunk. After all, I drank less today, as I always do before I go to a meeting. But they knew, all right. The message is beginning to sink in—*they* can do nothing to help me, unless *I* am serious about taking those first steps, proper steps, to help myself. You can't fox these people. It is one of the reasons why AA works. These people haven't just seen it all before, they have done it all themselves. They invented the lies I am trying to tell.

When I get home, I have a few more drinks to settle me down after the awful experience. In the morning I start the whole routine all over again. Sometime during the day it dawns on me that I heard someone in AA say that alcoholism is not just a disease, it is a *fatal* disease. Yet Alcoholics Anonymous is offering me treatment that will allow me to recover, though not be cured. Is my ego so big that I believe I can fight this disease all on my own? I carry on drinking through the day and yet I seem to need more alcohol than usual to bring me to the point where I don't feel the emotional pain any more.

The garden is green and smells of hot, wet earth, dampened by a glorious Transvaal thunderstorm that has washed away the heat and dust of the day, leaving the world cool and fresh.

I stand at the front door. The evening sun catches the drops of water on a spider's web and turns them into diamonds that glint and twinkle in the dying rays. Raindrops sparkle on the beautiful strands of silk spun between the flowerpot and the wall. There is a gentle breeze.

The big black spider sits ominously waiting on one side of the web, watching the little fly darting ever closer. Several times it seems as if the fly is about to land, but it suddenly changes direction and flies away to safety. And then it happens! It touches the sticky silk and is caught, fighting and desperate, in the spider's web.

The evening air is cool and yet I am hot, sweating, sick and hopeless. There can be no hope for me. I am an absolutely hopeless alcoholic. I have lost all self-respect and all dignity and I have nowhere to go and no one to turn to. Like the fly in the spider's web.

I remember my lost car and the equanimity with which those AA members let me walk away from their meeting. I see now that I have to take the first step. I have to admit that I am powerless over alcohol and that I need help. I turn my back on the spider and its web and walk inside.

I pick up the telephone and phone someone on the list of names and numbers that they gave me at one of the AA meetings I went to. The man lives down the road and I have known him for some time—our children went to the same school. I was deeply embarrassed when I first saw him at a meeting. It did not occur to me that he was there for the same reason I was.

I have to ask for help. I am not going to beat this disease on my own.

Pat comes immediately and sits and talks to Alex and me. I listen in horror as he says that he thinks that I ought to go into a rehabilitation clinic. He makes arrangements to meet me there early the next morning.

Alex washes his hands of the whole affair. "You're on your own," he says. "I have important meetings at work tomorrow and you must just get on with things as best you can." It seems to me that he is still able to ignore my plight.

I feel somewhat abandoned when I hear this. I am being left to face a huge crisis sick, shaking and on my own. Yet Alex's reaction is understandable. He does have important business meetings and probably feels that at this stage he can't afford to take time away from work to pay attention to me. Despite all my promises and my visits to the AA meetings, I have shown no signs of being able to overcome my alcoholism. Why should he think that I will be able to do it this time?

Before he leaves, Pat remarks, "Well, Alex, there is a bottle somewhere in this house, but we won't worry about that now." My hand flies to my handbag, where there is an inch or so of vodka left in a half-bottle. I drink it later that night and then throw the bottle away, convinced that I will never be able to do without alcohol in my life.

CHAPTER TWENTY-FOUR

THE REAL BEGINNING

It is early March, but already the leaves are falling from the oak trees, swirling around me in a blur of red and gold. The breeze is chilly and I have goose pimples from top to toe. I feel sick and I'm trembling, worse than those falling leaves have ever done. As I pace up and down, I wonder whether Pat will show up. I have no reason to believe that he won't keep his promise. I can hear the trains passing along the railway line behind me—behind the clinic—and I decide that if Pat has not arrived by 08:15, I will just go and lie down on the railway line and let the next train take care of things. Life is not worth living this way. Then I hear the sound of Pat's car and he is there, leading me gently and firmly down the path and into the clinic.

We enter the clinic and walk to the nurse's station. I freeze. Pat holds my elbow. I am trembling both inside and outside, not just with an alcoholic tremor but with sheer terror. What is going to happen to me here? In front of me stands the mayor's wife. We play bridge with her and her husband from time to time. The previous night's drinking has already made me flushed, but more blood rushes to my cheeks. Shame and embarrassment writhe in the pit of my stomach. Ann is not just the mayor's wife, she is also a nursing sister, and here she is on duty in the nurse's station at reception.

At that reception desk a new life began for me. It was there that I first encountered the gentle acceptance of my condition as a disease. Ann and her staff smiled at me with empathy and kindness. They explained that I suffered from an incurable disease, but that there was something I could do to recover from the dreadful state I was in and to start attending to the ruins of my past.

To my great relief they didn't have a bed for me in the clinic, and so I never went into rehab. I was given vitamin B and told to come back that night to attend an Alcoholics Anonymous meeting. The most successful rehab clinics teach the Twelve Steps programme and allow AA to hold meetings there.

I left the clinic and couldn't face a day alone at home. I made my way to the home of a very old friend and poured my heart out to her. Thank goodness she was understanding—and loving and kind—and suggested that I spend the rest of the day with her. I don't remember much about that day except that I knew I needed a drink to make me feel better, yet at last understood that a drink would make me sicker.

And so began the most important journey of my life. I knew that there would be rocks in the path and that the journey would not be easy, but I slowly began to realise that if I kept going to those meetings and did what the sober people there told me to do, there was, after all, hope and life to be found.

In the early days the craving for alcohol is difficult to deal with. So many people seem to think that one can "just stop" or that one should "pull oneself together". But addiction seems to put a stranglehold on one's self-control. I know that when I came to the end, when I knew that I needed help, I felt that I would die if I continued to drink—but that I would also die if I stopped. I had come to rely on alcohol to keep me going, to stop my early morning shakes, to keep me from vomiting first thing in the morning. How was I going to survive without it?

Yet survive I did. Many people struggle with the craving for alcohol for a long time after they have stopped drinking. But there are many of us who seem to have the craving for a drink removed from us almost straight away. I was one of those. I had the "heaves" in the early morning for a couple of weeks after I had had my last drink and I continued to tremble and shake for a while, but the craving for alcohol was completely removed from me.

One of the things that had dogged my drinking days was fear. I was afraid of everything and everyone and I continued to be fearful about many things in my life. It took a while of going to meetings and discussing these feelings with other members before I realised that I was not alone. We have all experienced dreadful fear and we have all had to deal with it. It is being with people who have experienced exactly what you have experienced that makes AA so useful and important.

Three weeks after I had stopped drinking we celebrated our silver wedding anniversary. We invited all our friends to a party, and our children came from school and university to be with us. That night I didn't crave alcohol, but I was dreadfully afraid of somehow picking up the wrong glass or having someone try to "spike" my drink as a joke. I kept watch over my glass all night and made sure that I poured my own drinks.

It was a wonderful party, yet I realised at the end of the evening that I had no idea whether Alex was pleased with me or not. I know now that it is just not easy for him to show his emotions. In the same way that he had appeared almost to ignore my drinking, he is able to take my sobriety for granted. In the same way that he didn't comment, or upbraid me when I was drunk, he doesn't compliment me for staying sober and unless I remind him of the anniversaries of my sobriety, he never comments on the fact that I have achieved another year without alcohol.

I know for sure today that this doesn't mean that Alex doesn't feel things—just that he is afraid of demonstrating his feelings. It explains the way he seemed to be able to live through the pain of my drinking without—except for one awful lapse—showing what was really going on in his heart and mind.

It surprised me when, about six months later, I told the managing director of the firm I was working for at the time that I had stopped drinking and was going to Alcoholics Anonymous. He looked at me with absolute amazement and declared that he had never known that I had a drinking problem and found it hard to believe. Such is the cunning of the alcoholic and the power of denial.

Many people today know about and use the Twelve Steps programme to help them recover from a variety of addictions. Alcoholics Anonymous created that powerful programme in

1935, and it was so successful that it spread around the world like wildfire.

For me, as with every recovering alcoholic, there was a lot to learn, but I was told to take it at my own pace and not to try to do everything at once. In the first months all I did was go to meetings and try to stay sober one day at a time. Gradually I made new friends. I learned to laugh with them and at myself.

I was armed with a number of telephone numbers and told to pick up the phone and call any one of them *before* I picked up a drink.

I was given AA literature and the Big Book (*Alcoholics Anonymous—the story of how many thousands of men and women have recovered from alcoholism*). I was told to read it regularly—especially if I couldn't sleep at night.

The way in which the people that I met at meetings cared about me kept me going along the difficult path to sobriety. Suddenly I found myself telling Alex what *we* were doing rather than what *they* were doing. That beautiful little prayer:

> *God grant me the serenity*
> *To accept the things I cannot change*
> *Courage to change the things I can*
> *And the wisdom to know the difference*

became my mantra. This prayer is said at AA meetings all over the world and is a very important part of one's recovery.

The words "Higher Power" and "God as I understand him" run like a shining thread through the programme of recovery from alcoholism. It took me a while to understand exactly what this means. At first I thought that I would need to become "religious" again. I had been very religious as a young girl, and the nuns at school had instilled in me a kind of spiritual awareness that had helped to keep me steady through the tumultuous days of my childhood. All aspects of that had vanished as I drank my way to death's door. I felt that God had abandoned me and that I would have to work very hard to get back into His good books.

I had kept going to church for a few years after the children were born, mainly because I knew that their father was an atheist and I felt that they needed some sort of spiritual guidance in their formative years. When they reached the stage where they could make up their minds for themselves, I lapsed into a kind of agnosticism myself and, until I found Alcoholics Anonymous, I abandoned all thoughts of spirituality or religion.

On joining the programme, I thought that it would be necessary for me to go back to church, and so I set off to visit the local Anglican priest. I told him that I was an alcoholic, at which point he crossed himself and said, "Let us pray for you, my dear," which he promptly did. I could no more pray at that stage than fly to the moon.

So began six months of "religiously" going to church each Sunday morning. People smiled at me and greeted me as I arrived and left the service, but no one ever made any effort to befriend me, to ask my name or to suggest that I join them for tea in the hall after the service. I never felt part of that church.

It was so different from AA meetings. At every meeting someone greeted me, asked me for my Christian name (we are anonymous, remember!), made sure to introduce me to someone else, made sure that I stayed for tea after the meeting and told me to please keep coming back to meetings. Most members see to it that every newcomer that comes through the doors of AA is welcomed and supported in this way. Those doors are always open and the people inside friendly and warm, empathetic rather than sympathetic. They know exactly what you are going through.

I learned not to compare my own experiences with those of others. Most importantly I learned the very important word "yet". I may not have drunken driving charges against me; I may not have been involved in dreadful car accidents; I may not have lost several jobs through my drinking, I may not have gone to jail—yet. And I was able to accept that, if I were to carry on drinking, I would certainly experience those things and more.

Something that was very important to me was that I found that there is no risk of judgement from anyone at an AA meeting, and that is what makes all AA members—and newcomers—feel safe and gives us the courage to share our experiences, strengths and hopes with each other.

I am told to get myself a sponsor, and my phone begins to ring. People phone to find out how I'm doing and there are always at least three calls the following day if I fail to attend my regular meeting. I start to laugh again and to feel some kind of awareness of the fact that I am a living creature worthy of the attention of others.

I stop going to church. No one phones me to find out why.

I have a very good friend who is an Anglican priest. I talk to him about my situation just after I have started taking AA seriously. He tells me that I am a sinner and should go to church. After a lot of self-seeking I give serious thought to what he said and I realise that if I am a sinner, then I have the choice to go to church. But alcoholism is not a sin and, if the place for sinners is church, the place for alcoholics is Alcoholics Anonymous. There is nowhere I feel more at home.

Two of my sons are deeply religious and the third is an atheist like his father. I go to church at Easter and Christmas and enjoy the atmosphere, the hymns and carols—and the sermons.

CHAPTER TWENTY-FIVE

NOT A RELIGIOUS PROGRAMME

At last I begin to tackle the difficult business of finding "a God of my understanding". I find this a very difficult concept to deal with at first. I don't believe in God any more. I have been told to find any concept that will work for me as a Higher Power, to seek spiritual things, spiritual understanding and spiritual growth and not worry about dogma and the church if I find the latter too difficult to embrace.

It is a cool and slightly overcast morning. I have taken a day's leave so that I can go to watch an international cricket match. I have been a lover of cricket since I was a little girl and my mother and I watched and scored for many games, including inter-provincials.

As I set off for the cricket ground, my packed lunch in my bag and my floppy white hat on my head, I listen to the car radio to get the latest score. The words hit me: "Rain has stopped play." Suddenly I am angry—angry at "fate", which has allowed it to rain on a day when I had especially contrived not to go to work so that I could watch cricket. I fume, I swear. I am almost in tears.

And then a calm comes over me. I don't know where it comes from, but the Serenity Prayer comes into my mind—"accept the things I cannot change". I feel a deep contentment and a deep joy at the same time. It dawns on me that, both literally and figuratively speaking, rain will stop play at certain times in my life for as long as I live. There are things I cannot change. Thunder, lightning, storms, drought, sunshine and wind will come and go, whether I like them or not, and I had better accept this fact pretty quickly or anger and disappointment will continue to be a part of my life.

Slowly I was beginning to find what I needed to keep going. Yet this new-found ability to accept whatever life threw at me didn't solve my problem with "a God of my understanding". I really wrestled with this idea until one night I was sitting in a meeting surrounded by my new friends, who had shown me that they loved me, cared about my sobriety and would help me in any way they could to achieve a serene and worthwhile way of living.

I wasn't listening too well to the speaker. My eyes were wandering over the faces of the people around me.

There was Susan, who had come back from the brink of death after a motor accident in which a child in the other car had been killed. Susie lives with the guilt to this day.

There was Paul, an advocate who had lost his job because of his drinking, but had clawed his way back through the programme of Alcoholics Anonymous to become one of the most sought-after advocates in the business.

Little Rick was there too, barely out of school, but in a bad way because of his drinking. He was sitting next to one of his teachers, who had brought him out of the darkness into AA and who phoned him every day and brought him to meetings every night.

The teacher himself had many years of sobriety and had come into the programme a physical wreck, having been hospitalised for "alcoleptic" fits. He was now at the top of his profession, loved and admired by his students. I looked at him and shook my head. This was the man from whom the nurses in the ward had fled when he had tried to light a cigarette. They were afraid that the fumes from the methylated spirits he had been drinking would ignite and set them all on fire.

As I looked around, I realised that it was these people who were keeping me sober, it was they who had literally saved my life. On that night GOD became for me a "Group Of Drunks". The love, care and compassion I got from my group settled in my mind as coming from a Group Of Drunks. It was a good beginning, and I have been on a path of spiritual growth ever since.

CHAPTER TWENTY-SIX

JOE DOESN'T GO AWAY

I fight my way up from the depths of sleep. I can hear shouting, raised voices, swearing. Oh God! It is Joe's turn to die and he has come to my house to do it.

Many years before this Joe developed a malignant growth behind the left eye. His eye was removed, but we always knew that the cancer could manifest itself somewhere else in the future. Joe wore a black patch over his left eye. He once made me smile about that patch and even led me to believe that somewhere in his heart he had some humanity. He had parked the car outside a country store and as he headed inside, a young child seated on the back of a light pick-up truck had shouted to him: "Are you a pirate?" to which Joe had immediately replied, in a swashbuckling tone: "Yes, I am!" The child had giggled. I thought I'd seen a twinkle in Joe's good eye. Was there something soft inside his heart after all?

Now the cancer has reappeared in kidney, liver, testicles and lungs. Joe moves his "residence" between my house and the homes of one of his sisters and his brother. As soon as one of us "offends" him in some way, he packs up his belongings and treks off to the next one on his list. I suppose it gives each of us some respite from his unpleasant nature and arrogant demands.

As I struggle into my dressing gown to go and investigate the reason for the shouting, I can hear the voice of the night nurse responding to Joe's abuse.

We decided to get a nurse in an attempt to give me some rest. Joe's demands both night and day are unreasonable, rude and most unpleasant. Joe is a racist of the worst kind and has turned against the black night nurse who is on duty. He is convinced that she is inefficient and not qualified to look after him. We have persevered for a few nights, but the situation is now worse than it was before we employed her.

As I enter Joe's room, the nurse is already packing her bag. She is apologetic about leaving but tells me that she has had enough and is not prepared to put up with such verbal abuse one minute longer. It is 02:30 in the morning, but she is determined to leave.

I persuade her to spend the rest of the night in the spare bedroom rather than venture out in the early hours of the morning. I sit in the easy chair in Joe's room and settle there for the rest of the night. My nostrils are filled with the sickly-sweet smell of the sick-room. I wonder just how long I am to be tortured by this man. I look at his sunken cheeks and thin, cruel mouth. I know that I have wished him dead many times and have even thought myself capable of killing him.

Yet at this moment I am desperately sorry for him. He is obviously close to death and entirely at my mercy—a complete role reversal. The time that comes for most parents, when they have to be cared for by their children, has come for Joe. I am quite unable to look on him as a father figure, yet I find it ironic that he is almost entirely dependent on me for his comfort and well-being. His eyelids flicker and he groans. I watch him as he drifts into an uneasy sleep. Then I too doze fitfully for a while, waking at intervals, checking on Joe and listening to the sounds of the night as my family sleep peacefully in their bedrooms in other parts of the house.

At six o'clock I bid the nurse farewell and pay her, adding a little extra to compensate her for all the unpleasantness she has had to endure.

And so begins a period of about two months, during which Joe insists on being ferried between my house and the homes of his brother and sister. He swears at us, complains about us and, as he grows weaker, becomes more and more obnoxious to us all.

During that time I had an ever-present memory of my mother walking along the rough dirt road of the little smallholding on which she and Joe lived to catch the bus about a mile away. Not once did Joe offer to drive her, and I suspect she was too afraid to ask. At the time my mother was the only one that brought any income into the marriage. They lived on what she earned.

Summer and winter, Mom walked that dusty road to catch the bus to school. She walked home again when the bus dropped her in the evenings after work. Sometimes it was dark and in winter it was always cold. Pretoria summers are humid and can be stiflingly hot. The summer thunderstorms for which Pretoria is known often drenched her to the bone. She was desperately afraid of lightning. When I was a little child she would sometimes drag us both under the bed during a thunderstorm. Why did no one ever suggest to Joe that he should give her a lift to and from the bus? Why didn't he think of doing it without being asked?

Why didn't I say something? How terribly afraid we all must have been of him that we allowed a brutal, vicious man like Joe to frighten us to the extent that we remained silent about his selfish and cruel behaviour.

During one of the times that Joe was staying with me while he was ill he said that he would like to make his will. We called a lawyer to come to the house and went out for the afternoon so that we would not be in the way or in any position to be accused of influencing him.

The day came when Joe's life was obviously fading, and he asked me in a weak voice if I would take him to the hospital where my mother had died so that he could end his days there.

We gently loaded him into the back of Alex's big car, propped up in a nest of cushions and blankets to make him comfortable, and drove him to the hospital in Pretoria. Early the next morning they phoned to tell me that he had died during the night.

It is impossible to describe what I felt. Relief was part of it, but I also felt sadness for all that had happened to us because of this man. I could not truly mourn him, yet he had been such a part of my life that there was a hole somewhere inside me that I couldn't account for.

People have asked me why I was willing to take this man into my home after the way he had made my life—and that of my mother—a misery. I can't really say, except that the programme of Alcoholics Anonymous teaches forgiveness. I believe that I was able to nurse Joe through his final illness because I knew that he was an alcoholic and, like me, he suffered from an incurable illness over which he had no control. I didn't have to like him but I needed to have compassion for him. Above all, I know that I now see both Joe and my mother as unfortunate alcoholics, who never found the way out that I have found. I have learned that alcoholism is a disease and not a moral problem.

At his funeral one of Joe's sisters came to me and said: "Don't worry, Jean, Joe and your mother are together again." Thank goodness for my aunt, who promptly whispered in my ear: "Expect your mother at the door when you get home tonight!" Whoever said that laughter is the best medicine knew what he was talking about!

Later we found that Joe had left all he had to me, with some smaller amounts to the brother and sister who had helped to nurse him. The amount he left was not large, but his family nevertheless tried to contest the will. The lawyer who had drawn it up had a great deal to say about that, and eventually the contest was withdrawn. I have never seen Joe's family or heard from them since.

CHAPTER TWENTY-SEVEN

ALCOHOLICS ANONYMOUS

I still go to Alcoholics Anonymous meetings regularly. We talk about "working" the AA programme of recovery and, indeed, that is exactly what one needs to do, really put hard work and commitment into one's recovery. I found that what they had told me was true: "The programme is simple, but not easy." I went to as many meetings as I could, sitting in a variety of church halls, library meeting rooms and school halls, listening as carefully as I could. Most of the halls were uncomfortably filled with smoke. My eyes burned and watered and I came home with my clothes and hair smelling so badly of smoke that I could have been a smoker myself. I remember wondering if I was going to die of lung cancer sooner than I would have died of drink! Luckily today there is no smoking in AA meetings any more.

Going to meetings almost every night meant that I was out of the house at night almost as much as I had been during the time that I was drinking. Partners of alcoholics find it difficult to come to terms with this when the alcoholic sobers up. It must be difficult for them to believe that you have to be at meetings almost every night at first, that you hang on to the support and understanding that you find in those meetings, and that you have to learn how to apply the Twelve Steps to your life.

I knew that this programme was going to save my life. For me that didn't just mean that I was not going to die from drinking but also that I could change my entire life, find a new direction and take steps that would completely change me and the way I lived my life.

It took about a year before I began to feel better about myself. It was not just the programme that worked for me but also being with people who had travelled the same tortured path that I had, and who understood that I don't have a moral problem but that I suffer from a disease. I took greater care with my appearance. I had more money to spend on clothes and cosmetics and I took pride in looking as good as I could.

I also began to play the piano again. Music and playing the piano had been an important part of my life and I now found that sitting at the keys, making music, was therapeutic and helped me to realise that there were things that I could do and it really didn't matter if I wasn't good at doing them. After a short while I decided to take lessons in syncopation and found that I was quite good. What a joy it was to be able to make music once more, and being able to play made an important contribution to my sobriety. I spent many hours just playing for my own enjoyment, and the music soothed my soul as I ventured further along the road to recovery.

It is the first anniversary of my sobriety. As it is my AA "birthday", I have been asked to choose my own chairman and speakers for the meeting. There's a proper birthday cake on the table, complete with one candle—not childish, but childlike, rather. As the lights in the hall are switched off, I light the candle. A small flame flickers into life and I am filled with a sense of complete disbelief. A year ago no one would have convinced me that I would be able to stay away from alcohol for a whole year.

The next morning, one year plus one day down the line, I realise that all I have to do is to stop for one day at a time, just as I have managed during the previous year.

I also understand that the disease of alcoholism is incurable and that I will be an alcoholic for the rest of my life. The good news is that it is a treatable disease and, as long as I can stay away from taking that first drink, I will remain sober.

CHAPTER TWENTY-EIGHT

ROCKS IN THE ROAD

After three years of sobriety Alex and I found that we had drifted completely apart. At first he had seemed supportive, but gradually AA seemed to take over my life altogether, without leaving any time for him. Balance—this is something that all of us in the programme have to learn: to make space for ourselves as well as our families and our jobs. Yet it is very important for the family to understand that nothing is going to get better or return to "normal" if the alcoholic doesn't embrace the programme and remain sober. Many husbands and wives feel resentful of the fact that "strangers" have helped their partners to get sober, while they appear to have been unable to do this.

It was not only meetings that took me out of the house. One of the most important ingredients of an AA member's recovery is working with still suffering alcoholics, carrying to them the message of recovery, sharing our new-found strength and hope. By doing this, we help ourselves to stay sober, and I was involved in this as part of my own recovery.

I learned more about this "disease of denial" during the earlier days of my sobriety. I was asked to visit a woman who had called the AA office and asked for help. I knocked at her front door. It was opened by her husband. I told him that I had come to see his wife, and he asked me in. I found her sitting on the couch. She looked awful. Her skin was yellow, her eyes had no sparkle—in fact, she looked half dead. I took her hands and told here that I was an alcoholic and had come to try to help her.

At that point her husband reacted with great anger. He grabbed me by the arm and dragged me away from his wife. "How dare you?" he shouted. "My wife is not an alcoholic. Why are you here, interfering in our lives?" I told him that his wife had phoned and asked for help. He couldn't believe it and rounded on her. She was quietly crying by this time. I asked him why he thought his wife had phoned AA for help if she didn't feel that she had a drinking problem. He had no answer to that and asked me to leave.

I left that house very sad and wondered how long it would take for him to accept that his wife needed help. The chances were that she would die of the disease before he was prepared to let her get help.

There is a wonderful "sister" organisation to AA, called Alanon, where partners and family of alcoholics can go to share their experiences and learn to understand that alcoholism is a disease. Many of these people end up as sick as the alcoholic, and need to talk to others who have been through the same suffering. Alanoners are a joyful group, and many have learned to live happy and useful lives, even if their partners have not yet stopped drinking. Alex consistently refused to go to Alanon meetings.

The time came when Alex felt that he couldn't even talk to me without "throwing my alcoholism in my face". Those were the words he used when I suggested that we discuss a situation that had slowly become untenable over the previous three years. And it is those words that stay with me today, reminding me of the fact that Alex will always be undemonstrative and unable either to confront demons or celebrate miracles. He was as incapable of bringing up the subject of our having drifted apart as he was of talking to me about my alcoholism. I know for sure that he cares about me and he has always been someone of whom I am enormously proud. I also suspect that he prefers to let me have my way rather than cause controversy between us.

I felt it best to move out of the house. I found a charming little cottage not far from where I worked and settled there. There was a small but pretty garden, with bougainvillea growing around the front door. I planted two hundred daffodils in that garden, which resulted in an absolute riot of waving yellow blooms. I felt, as I watched them, that they must rival Wordsworth's "host of golden daffodils".

In the meanwhile, the partner of one of my friends at AA insisted that Alex go to an Alanon meeting—something he had previously refused to do. He learned a lot there and came to understand more about the disease. He phoned me and said, "They gave me a book to read, and it was written about you."

Our sons were shocked and very unhappy, yet they showed us both support and understanding. Something for which I have the utmost gratitude is that my drinking didn't destroy my relationship with my children. All three my sons are supportive and interested in my recovery and the programme of AA. They express pride in me too. The two eldest were at university in Cape Town when I joined AA and so did not feel deprived by my being out of the house at AA meetings so often. The youngest was still at boarding school.

However, neither Alex nor I was content to be apart. For me it was a lonely time. I missed my home and I missed my husband. After several months we managed to talk to each other honestly, and eventually I moved back home with him. He continued to go to Alanon meetings for several years, and this was something which helped us to mend our relationship.

By his own admission, his attendance at Alanon meetings helped Alex too. He found that he was not alone in what he had gone through; that, in fact, there were many people who had suffered the same things—and sometimes things that were worse than what he had endured. Alanon uses the same Twelve Steps programme that AA does and the help and support that its members get from each other have helped to mend many relationships and bring happiness and trust back into the lives of those who go there.

CHAPTER TWENTY-NINE

GOING FORWARD

There was often laughter to be found in certain situations. I didn't share the fact that I am an alcoholic with many people at first and certainly not with my husband's business friends and acquaintances. One of my favourite memories of the early days of my sobriety is of attending a business banquet. As usual, I turned my wine glass upside down and the waiter removed it when I ordered a soft drink.

The stranger sitting next to me exclaimed at the fact that I wasn't going to have any wine. He started to get quite pushy about it, to the point of being rather unpleasant. Eventually he found another wine glass and poured a very small amount of wine into it. He handed it to me, saying, "Come on, you don't know what you are missing!"

I couldn't control my laughter. It was all I could do not to point out to the young fellow that I had probably drunk more wine in the last year of my drinking days than he had in his entire life.

Very often the people who urge you most strongly to have alcohol, who try to make you feel that you are out of step with the rest of the world, tend to be very heavy or even problem drinkers themselves.

Now that I was sober, my working life also improved. I began to feel that I could probably take steps to improve my position, but my performance had improved so much that other people noticed it too. Before I could take any steps, I was offered a position on the board of a large company.

I was dreadfully afraid of failure, but I took the job and decided to throw my heart and soul into it. When I moved into my office on the first day, I was trembling on the inside, but those shaky hands had long since disappeared. I was so frightened that I nearly rushed into the MD's office and told him that I couldn't manage the job! If I had ever felt that I was not "good enough", this was the moment! But I managed, just as I managed all aspects of my new life—"one day at a time".

I laugh as I stand at the sink in the little kitchen. I am washing dishes quite late in the evening after having conducted a focus group. Joan, my friend and personal assistant, has just grumbled good-naturedly that she actually goes out to work so that she doesn't have to wash dishes. And now, here she is at half past eight at night, still in the office—and washing dishes.

My feet ache, and I'm sure that Joan's do too. The water is hot and sudsy and I enjoy the feel of it on my hands, the lemon smell of it and the sight of the cups coming out of the water clean and shining.

I have started my own business! Several years after I started that new job with such fear and trepidation, I have launched out on my own. Doing so is a huge leap of faith for me. And I don't really believe that I can do this!

It is tough and it is hard work. I "sell" my services as hard as I can, which isn't easy, because I don't have much faith in my abilities. Every time I hand a report to a client, I am sure that it is really just "luck" that has brought me here.

An ex-colleague is my financial backer. He wanted me to choose very expensive furniture and fittings. He comes from an advertising agency background, where everything has to be avant-garde and expensive. Joan and I scoured the cheaper places for our office furniture and we seem to have made a really good job of it too. It is just as well that we did, because within six months it becomes obvious that my "backer" is going bankrupt!

I hastily find someone to take over my "debt", and we set about working hard to pay it off. The business grows and grows and becomes ever more successful. I can't believe that I have managed to establish a successful small business, which in time has become a force to be reckoned with in the industry.

I give the business my full attention, making sure that I stay away from the first drink, one day at a time, going to meetings and trying to help others who suffer from the disease of alcoholism. People in AA tell many stories of successful achievements, of managing to study for degrees, even doctorates, of finding that, because they give themselves completely to the programme of recovery, they are able to pull themselves out of the mire into which their alcoholism has driven them.

CHAPTER THIRTY

GETTING THERE

Our sons went to university, brought home a variety of girlfriends and generally did the things that good and loving sons do. My alcoholism seemed to fade into the past. I could meet all the girls with a sober heart and mind and didn't embarrass anyone! The feeling of being sober and accepted is something that never leaves one. Being able to accept into the family people who had never seen me drunk was—and still is—an absolute joy. In AA meetings all over the world one hears recovered alcoholics talk about how grateful they are to have children and grandchildren, colleagues and friends, who have never seen them drunk.

I have talked with my sons about the time that I was drinking. I was amazed to hear from one of them that he had never thought of me as being an alcoholic—yes, he had known that I was drinking too much. Then after I got sober he read an article in a magazine—an interview with a woman who was an alcoholic. He did not realise that the interview was with me until he read the account of how I used to lace a jug of orange juice with gin or vodka and keep it in the fridge, thinking that no one would know that I wasn't drinking pure orange juice when I poured myself a glass from the jug. One day, to my horror, my son came to tell me that he had thrown out the orange juice "because it tasted horrible".

It was only upon reading the article that he realised that the person being interviewed was me and that I was, indeed, an alcoholic. It wasn't a word he cared to use. Nobody does.

The bank manager has a smarmy smile on his face. If I squeeze him, I am sure I will get snake oil on my fingers. His office is hot and my arms stick to the vinyl of the chair. My son Dan's wife is all but growling at him and the rage and frustration that we both feel are tangible in the air around us.

The Bophuthatswana government has ordered the bank to freeze Dan's account, and ordered the post office to hold his mail. Penny and I have come to see if we can do anything to make the bank free up his funds and get the post office to give us his mail. Payments from the medical aid companies are not getting through and the bank won't allow him to use his account. The sister in his medical practice needs to be paid, so do the rent and the cleaner and a host of other bills. Dan is unable to travel to Bop because he has been deported, and so his wife and I take on the bank manager and the post office—and, in the end even the security police—to see what we can do.

But our hands are tied and we find that there is really nothing we can do—except make the rotund bank manager feel somewhat uncomfortable in the face of our relentless accusations and a rather spectacular show of our disapproval, which, in my case at least, borders on hatred.

Like me, Dan has always taken an interest in political issues. After qualifying as a doctor he went to practise in Bophuthatswana. There he inevitably became embroiled in the politics of the day. It was the mid-eighties, and there was a state of emergency in the country. As a result of his reporting evidence of severe torture in one of the local prisons, he had been first detained and then deported and his practice closed down.

The rooms where Dan once practised are musty, and we sense they have not been inhabited for some time. The electricity has been cut off, and it is dark and chilly and rather spooky. The sound of our footsteps on the wooden floor echoes around us.

After our fruitless battle with the bank manager Penny and I have come to clear up and take back to South Africa everything we can fit into the Kombi borrowed for the purpose.

We manage to salvage a host of things: an old and charming wooden bench, which we later learn was one of the original benches in the first school in what was then known as Mafeking, now Mafikeng. The rooms are in part of the old school building. We cram the big office chair into the back of the Kombi together with—this makes us giggle—about a year's worth of contraceptive pills, which will save friends and family a lot of money. Panado, too, will take away our headaches for several months to come.

The whole experience is stressful and hurtful and causes us both great anxiety. We pile everything we can into the Kombi and set out glumly. We are mightily relieved as we cross the border back into South Africa.

As we leave Bop, we come across a beautiful field of pink and white cosmos alongside the road. I slam on the brakes and we leap out of the vehicle and set about picking armfuls of the flowers, the sun warm on our backs. As we step amongst the flowers, the sound of the crickets stop and all we can hear is the traffic flying by on the tarred road next to us. We frolic and sing and shout and dance with the sheer joy of being out of that hateful place, even though we have only managed to save a handful of Dan and Penny's possessions. Once we have packed the cosmos into the back of the Kombi, we set off for Johannesburg: a little subdued, very thoughtful and absolutely exhausted.

This particular day stands out in my memory as a milestone. Friends have asked me why. Being able, in my sobriety, to give emotional support to my family and even, as in this case, to provide supportive action on their behalf make me grateful beyond belief. I used to be such an ineffectual creature, a worry and a burden to my family, that sober and effective support of this nature is a way of making amends to them.

Being able to be there to support Dan and his wife was a joy to me and was another thing that I would never have been able to do if I had still been drinking. My sons had always accepted quite calmly the fact that I was going to AA. They probably felt happy and relieved that I was on the path to recovery. Part of the AA programme requires making amends to those we have harmed during our drinking. I have tried to do this with my sons and my husband. But the best way that I can make amends, I believe, is by staying sober and being the best mom I can be each day.

CHAPTER THIRTY-ONE

SEEING STARS

Panic overtook me as I stepped out of the telephone booth. My pretty paisley-patterned purse was gone. It must have been snatched from under my nose as I was phoning my cousin in Los Angeles. My heart beat hard in my chest and I felt light-headed. I couldn't deal with this. I was sure that I had put the purse on the little ledge under the phone, but when I turned to collect it, it was gone. Someone must have stolen it while my back had been turned. I never saw it again.

But of course I could deal with it. I was no longer an active alcoholic. I had a programme that helped me to deal with any kind of situation without having to use alcohol. I could make choices now and I knew what was the right thing to do.

This was my first trip to the United States. I was on a business trip to New York, visiting the offices of an advertising agency there to bring back some new ideas to put to the test in South Africa.

I couldn't believe my luck when I realised that the Alcoholics Anonymous World Convention was being held in

New Orleans in the same month. I had counted my money (which was no longer being spent on vodka and gin) and found that I could manage to fly from New York to New Orleans and then to Los Angeles, where one of my cousins lives.

More than 28 000 alcoholics gathered in New Orleans, and there was not a spot of bother from any of them. I tried to picture the mayhem that might have occurred had we all been in the heyday of our drinking years!

All over the city there were notices saying "Welcome to AA", and the bars and restaurants offered special alcohol-free cocktails. It was there that I learned that a cocktail without alcohol is called a "virgin" cocktail. Riding in the hotel lift one day, I thought I was very clever when I asked if a Bloody Mary without the vodka was called a Virgin Mary. "No, Ma'am," came the reply from the back of the lift, "it's called a Bloody Shame!"

On the Fourth of July, in the large park in the middle of New Orleans, I dance and sing and follow the floats in the Mardi Gras. I am having the time of my life. The noise is unbelievable as everyone dances and sings. Somewhere in the park there is a fireworks display, sending rockets and fountains of coloured stars fizzing up into the sky, leaving a smell of gunpowder in the air. I am not afraid of the fireworks this time. People kiss complete strangers and masked ladies throw AA medallions into the crowd from the back of the floats. I fall down on the grass and lie there laughing. I see stars above me and I realise that during the time that I was drinking I had not been able to see the stars. I had usually passed out or fallen asleep some place where the stars were hidden from me anyway and I wouldn't have been able to see them even if I had been awake. Stars are beautiful.

I don't neglect the tourist attractions and take myself off—together with hundreds of other recovered alcoholics—to Bourbon Street, where I listen to jazz bands and walk in the narrow cobbled streets overlooked by balconies sporting "broekie lace"—the wonderfully complicated wrought iron work that graces the whole of Bourbon Street. (As I write this, Bourbon Street is a wreck and the whole of the city of New Orleans has been virtually wiped out by Hurricane Katrina. I have such special memories of being sober and happy in New Orleans that it is hard to visualise—or believe—what it must look like now.)

I even take a trip on a Mississippi river boat without once feeling that I might lurch and fall overboard!

On the Saturday night there is the Big Meeting in the New Orleans Superdome, an edifice so big that more than 28 000 of us fill only about half of it! I hear an ex-airline pilot tell how he piloted a plane while he was drinking. When the powers-that-be cottoned on to this, they transferred him to air traffic control! How little understanding employers have of this disease! Not to mention the man in the street.

Alcoholics of all nationalities, all sizes, all persuasions and with long, short and in-between years of sobriety, shared their experiences, strengths and hopes with the huge and happy crowd. We laughed a lot together—it was the kind of "giddy" laughter born out of enjoyment. As one of my AA friends recently said, "That kind of giddiness in sobriety is one of the real positives (of being sober) and there is no wonky memory or recriminations in the morning."

What a wonderful time I had for those few days, and all without having to drink any alcohol at all. I had thought it impossible to have fun without alcohol. I learned during those days in New Orleans that I had friends all over the world, who understood me and loved me. I spent hours in meetings, hours talking to people with whom I could identify, people who knew that I was not immoral but sick. People who empathised with me, who had done the same things that I had done and had forgiven themselves for those actions.

Ten years later I went to another World Convention, this time in Seattle. And once again I was overwhelmed by the sheer size of it, by the huge numbers of alcoholics from all over the world that attended, by the camaraderie and love in the air. And this time I also realised—because of the delighted welcome that we received from the city—how different AA Conventions are. No drunken brawls, no theft, few breakages, much laughter, lots of smiles and an air of gratitude that is almost palpable.

I have found friends all over the world and have managed to travel to many countries where I have attended meetings and where people that I have never seen before have welcomed me as their friend and treated me as a member of their family.

CHAPTER THIRTY-TWO

MILESTONES

"Hi, everybody, my name is Jean and I am an alcoholic." So I have introduced myself at hundreds of meetings. I am doing so again at this, my tenth anniversary of sobriety. My family are all here: sons and daughters-in-law, the friend with whom I spent my first day of sobriety, my husband and, of course, all my good and loving friends in AA.

The ten candles on my cake cast their soft glow into the room, where the lights have been lowered. The light caused by ten candles is so much brighter than that cast by only one. Yet we never forget in AA that we live our lives one day at a time. We cannot change yesterday and have no control over what will happen tomorrow. We stop drinking only one day at a time. There is such significance in that cake with the candles, and the anniversaries of my sobriety have come to mean more to me than the anniversaries of my birth.

Early the following morning my phone rings. It is my eldest son to tell me that his wife has given birth to a baby girl. I laugh as I realise that that young girl attended her first AA meeting as an unborn child.

Fifteen years later she will come up to me—on my twenty-fifth AA anniversary—and say some of the sweetest words I have ever heard.

The room is buzzing as people chat amongst themselves and move the chairs away to make room for the coffee and cake. The meeting is over and I am elated and full of gratitude. I smell coffee being poured in the kitchen and it reminds me of scores o similar occasions in the past.

Suddenly two of my granddaughters are in front of me, standing to attention on the other side of the cloth-covered table. One of them attended her last AA meeting before she was born fifteen years ago.

"We've come to a decision," they say in unison.

"Oh," I ask, "and what is that?"

"You're a cool gran," comes the answer.

The lump hits my throat immediately and I swallow to stop the tears. What a gift they are giving me. I could not have hoped for anything better. I look at the two bright, smiling faces before me. Blonde hair and blue eyes and a sprinkling of freckles, like chocolate on the top of cappuccino foam.

Oh, how sweet it is to be a cool gran, and I suspect that it is good, at the age of fifteen, to have such a cool gran too.

And how sweet it is to be surrounded by people who are celebrating with me because they know the importance of this occasion, people who love me and believe that I am good enough.

CHAPTER THIRTY-THREE

"KEEP COMING BACK"

I still put out the chairs at the meetings, I empty and wash coffee cups and I try to greet any newcomer to the rooms of AA, just to try to make them feel less afraid and miserable. Newcomers are easily spotted because they have lifeless eyes. Very often they are also shaking uncontrollably, some are crying and they are almost always terrified.

They are always made welcome. The people in the rooms of AA know where they have come from, what they are feeling, how afraid they are. New people are always told that if they have a drinking problem they have come to the right place. No one will ever tell them that they are alcoholics. This is something they need to decide for themselves, and they will learn how to make this decision while they are in the rooms of AA. They are always told to "keep coming back".

I thank God that I kept going back.

I have also, over the years, managed to offer service to the fellowship at a national and international level. This is no more important than washing the cups and making the coffee.

In AA we believe that doing service is an important part of staying sober, and I have certainly found this to be true.

The programme of recovery as offered by AA is firmly based on spiritual principles. In 2005 there was an AA presence in over 180 countries around the world.

When I started writing this, the memory of a young girl hiding behind a curtain was strong in my mind. I have told my story because I am Jean and I am an alcoholic and I hid behind the curtain for many years. At the beginning of the story I hid from Joe and the threat he posed. My shyness and lack of self-worth put up a curtain between me and the world, between me and my family, and I allowed the curtain to grow more opaque and heavier as time went by. Using alcohol put the final lining to it and cut me off completely from the world around me: a world that I avoided for more than half my life.

I know that there are people out there behind curtains of their own. After peeping out from behind mine and being helped to draw it back and see myself as good enough to take my place in the world, I would like to think that my story might help just one person to peep out from behind his or her curtain and take the hand that Alcoholics Anonymous offers.

CHAPTER THIRTY-FOUR

LIFE IS GOOD

The music is from the 1950s. Friends and family are all around me. I have seven grandchildren now, four girls and three boys, and none of them has ever seen me drunk. I feel intense gratitude when I realise I could have been dead or in an institution because of my drinking but, instead, I have the privilege of seeing these children growing up strong and beautiful and loving.

And I can see that they love me tonight. A lamb is gently revolving over the coals outside and the aroma tantalises the taste buds. Candles are flickering in dark-blue holders on the veranda and old friends and all the family are here, smiling and happy.

There is no fear in my life tonight, no feeling of guilt or inadequacy.

I look up and see my brother-in-law. What is he doing here? Perhaps he is out from England for a business meeting with his family. And then I spot my sister and behind her my brother. They have travelled all the way from the UK to be with us on this particular day—the day on which I turn seventy and just three days after Alex and I celebrated our golden wedding anniversary. Fifty years through thick and thin—I can hardly believe it! This evening we are celebrating both events with a spit braai for our special friends and family.

I can't believe that my brother and sister and her husband have come all that way just to be with us tonight. I find that the rest of my family have all been party to the secret and have managed to keep it from me successfully right up until the moment that they put in an appearance at the party.

I feel tears behind my eyes and I step off the veranda onto the lawn. I raise my eyes to the heavens and see that all curtains have been drawn back and the sky, like my heart, is full of stars.

There is no feeling in the world that beats being sober.

To contact AA in South Africa:
Johannesburg: (011) 683-9101
Cape Town: (021) 510-2288
Durban: (031) 301-4959
East Rand: (011) 421-1534
Port Elizabeth (041) 585-3626
Pretoria (012) 331-2446

For information worldwide go to
http://www.alcoholics-anonymous.org/?Media=PlayFlash